Awakening the Heart

*Discover Your True Capacity for Joy,
Inner Peace and Boundless Love*

Paul Dugliss, M.D.

© Copyright New World Ayurveda, LLC doing business as The Dugliss Institute - All rights reserved.

The content within this book may not be reproduced, duplicated or transmitted without direct written permission from the author or the publisher. Under no circumstances will any blame or legal responsibility be held against the publisher, or author, for any damages, reparation, or monetary loss due to the information contained within this book, either directly or indirectly. You are responsible for your own choices, actions, and results.

Legal Notice:

This book is copyright protected. This book is only for personal use. You cannot amend, distribute, sell, or use the content within this book, without the consent of the author or publisher.

Disclaimer Notice:

Please note the information contained within this document is for educational and entertainment purposes only. All effort has been expended to present accurate, up-to-date, and reliable, complete information. No warranties of any kind are declared or implied. Readers acknowledge that the author is not engaging in the rendering of legal, financial, medical or professional advice. The content within this book has been derived from various sources. Please consult a licensed professional before attempting any techniques outlined in this book. By reading this document, the reader agrees that under no circumstances is the author responsible for any losses, direct or indirect, which are incurred as a result of the use of the information contained within this document, including, but not limited to, — errors, omissions, or inaccuracies.

Contents

Introduction ~ There is More Under Heaven and Earth   1

Chapter 1 ~ A Vision of Possibilities   9

Chapter 2 ~ The Dilemmas of the Mind   23

Chapter 3 ~ Expanding Awareness & The Fullness of the Heart   35

Chapter 4 ~ Awakening the Heart   59

Chapter 5 ~ The Doors of Perception: Awe at the Miracle of Life   75

Chapter 6 ~ The Peace that Passeth Understanding: Radical Acceptance   99

Chapter 7 ~ The Bliss: Unconditional Joy   119

Chapter 8 ~ The One Heart: Complete Forgiveness and Compassion   133

Conclusion ~ Your Relationship with Universal Love   155

Contemplations ~ The Facets of the Heart   163

Final Words ~ Keep Your Light Shining Brightly   181

Resources ~ Growing through the Path of Love   183

My greatest wish for you is that you discover how amazing you are and know you are loved.

May it be so.

Acknowledgements

The great blessing of this life has been the amazing friends and teachers I have learned from over the years. I do not claim ownership of these teachings as these Universal truths have come from them, and it is my privilege to be sharing them with you. Deepest gratitude and credit to David McClanahan, who has guided and fostered my growth and whose teachings have inspired so much of this book. It is with a full heart that I acknowledge my other teachers and friends, especially Laszlo Sute, Janice Kinney, Charlie Lutes, Aureya Magdalen, Verlyn McGilvray, and my dear brother Bill, who was instrumental in inspiring my early seeking for truth. Great appreciation for my editor, Keziah Daniel. Her intuitive wisdom has been invaluable in helping bring forth this work. Great appreciation and gratitude to all my students and friends who have supported me in bringing this knowledge forward—your support has meant everything to me.

Finally, great love and gratitude to my wife, Sandra, for supporting me in bringing this wisdom to the world.

Introduction

There is More Under Heaven and Earth

The business and method of mysticism is Love. —*Evelyn Underhill*

Truly understanding the depth of Love is perhaps the best-kept secret in our current age. The tremendous power we hold as human beings—the power to move mountains—is within each of us and yet remains untapped. Why? Because we live mostly from the head and not the heart; the mind diminishes Love, the greatest force of the Universe, to a mere "feeling."

It is the illusion of the mind that says love can be impractical and "too romantic." Because love affects our emotional state profoundly, we think of it as a feeling. But feelings are from our animal heritage, they are hormonal reactions. This is clear when we consider our intense feelings in the fight-or-flight reactions to danger. Love is so much more. When we begin to understand love as a Universal Power that is accessible to each of us through our own awakened heart, then we open up to greater understanding.

Most of us would say that love is one of, if not the most important thing in our lives. If that is the case, why don't we know how to work with it and develop it? What better education and practice is there to engage in?

If you desire success in life—if you want to live 1000 percent of life—the synergy of the spiritual and the material—then the first thing you must do is recognize how to cultivate the heart. Doing so allows us to know the true nature of reality.

One way to fathom and contain the vast mystery of Universal Love is to look at the experience of its Masculine and Feminine aspects. The heart-centering approach we will explore and experience in this book incorporates both the Masculine path of knowing consciousness and developing awareness, as well as the Feminine path of unity through compassion, nurturance, and creative expression. We want to have both aspects fully developed—silent, peaceful being and blissful, creative flow.

The fullness of the Feminine nurturing ease and grace is too often missed and is in great need of development at this time. Evelyn Underhill, author of one of the most acclaimed books on mysticism, made the point that Love is the business and method of mysticism, which is coming to know "the mystery," attaining the knowledge of Reality. Outside of Rumi and Underhill, we have too few well-known examples of those who have emphasized the Feminine aspect of Universal Love. Of those who have explored and so beautifully given voice to a way of inner development based on love, too few are known and even fewer have been truly heard. While this book discusses consciousness as an important context, it seeks to give voice and illuminate the path to the Feminine aspects of Universal Love.

Regardless of the path you are on, whatever spiritual practice you engage in, whatever inner growth you're seeking, whatever you are wanting to heal within you, whatever religion or beliefs you follow, whatever mission you are on, whatever goal you seek, whatever suffering you want to leave behind, you will be so well served by awakening the heart and coming to know the treasure that it is. This is basic education, essential adult human development. The most efficient methods for awakening the heart are to be known and practiced in order to uplift all of humanity. Now, what does awakening the heart mean?

I remember part of this service I attended as a young man, "Thou shalt love the Lord thy God with all thy heart, and all thy soul, and all thy mind. This is the first and greatest commandment. And the second is like unto it; Thou shalt love thy neighbor as thyself. On these two commandments hang all the Law and the Prophets." I heard this. I understood. But I was left with the question, "How in the world can I ever do this?" Especially when I didn't have any direct experience of God and was beginning to question if what I was being taught was real. The second part was particularly difficult for me as I didn't love myself very much, and I didn't want to treat my neighbor the way I treated myself anyway. I did not understand that what was being taught needed to be supplemented with growth and greater awareness.

Awakening the heart means expanding direct awareness of the subtle energy of Universal Love. It means living and integrating all the qualities and aspects that flow spontaneously from that foundational awareness. This is a horse-and-cart issue. The usual approach puts thought first and then tries to drag the emotions, attitudes, perceptions, and habits along with it, often through will power and discipline. This is putting the cart before the horse. When we experience the fullness of the Universal or Spiritual Heart, we cannot help but experience, and therefore know, the qualities and aspects of it. I have termed these aspects the "Facets of the Heart." When we awaken the heart, these qualities unfold authentically in our lives, this is the ease of the Feminine aspect of Love. The Facets of the Heart that will unfold in your lived experience include:

Radical acceptance, unshakeable faith, loving presence, grace, inner guidance, unconditional joy, true appreciation, gratitude, generosity, radiance healing, total forgiveness, and full compassion.

Awakening the heart, as we will learn about in this book, dramatically accelerates inner growth, relieves suffering, and transforms one's life into a joyous and unique expression of our inherent Divinity.

Although these statements may seem bold, I have stood witness to the transformation of so many lives through the power of awakening the heart, that for me it is an understatement.

The hope with this writing is that it can be the beginning of a bold transformation and a call for a new approach to life, success, and spirituality. An approach not based on belief or ritual, but on the experience of the most powerful force in the Universe.

The point of this book is not for you to believe any of this; it is to inspire you to learn how to cultivate the heart. I want you to experience something beyond the most profound love you could imagine. I want you to discover within yourself hidden powers and potentials you never knew existed. I want you to journey to the center of your Universe and unfold the secrets that have eluded so many for so long.

So perhaps you have been looking, Dear Reader, in all the wrong places for the joy, bliss, fulfillment, love, and peace you deserve. When, with all compassion and deep understanding, the spiritual teachers say to look within, they are pointing to the way. But as I asked myself in that service I attended as a young man, "How?" With what tool? How do we look within? Where do we look?

It is quite difficult to conceive of, but the ability to use more of the tool we call the brain—that is what is needed and what is absolutely possible. A deeper understanding of the mind and psychology is needed if we are to become aware of the heart. A different use of this tool we call our brain.

Your journey to the heart can be short, and the suffering can be gone, and bliss, awe, and joy can be the essence of life going forward. For to quote Shakespeare: "There is more under Heaven and Earth than in your philosophy, Horatio."

Feel the call to this "more under Heaven and Earth" within your own heart. Feel into this call and how it tends to draw you. And like an ember, fan that into a fire that propels you into the ocean of Universal Love.

I invite you to discover the transformative power of Universal Love through the awakening of your own heart. With gratitude I share this message and method that has come not from me, but through me.

All Love, Light and Blessings,
Dr. Paul

Chapter 1

A Vision of Possibilities

In 1996 Jill Bolte Taylor was a healthy 37-year-old neuroanatomist at Harvard. She knew the brain and its function intellectually. But one morning that year, she was about to know the right brain most intimately. Jill had a stroke that wiped out much of her left brain. She was unable to walk, talk, read, write, or remember her past.

This was the irony of ironies—a neuroanatomist unable to describe her direct experience of the right brain, which she had studied intensely and taught.

Horrible, you might think. Yet strangely enough, she later describes this experience as euphoric. She experienced tranquility, safety, blessedness and omniscience.. It was so blissful and expansive that she wondered how her spirit could ever fit back in her body.

So here is a scientist who was able to perceive reality through the right brain without the dominant left brain thinking, interfering, or overriding what she was experiencing. Her left-brain dominance had been removed, and she was able to perceive reality unbound from the influence of the past, unconstrained by concepts and old associations. She noted that thirty years of emotional baggage was wiped out in seconds, as if healed instantly by the awe-inspiring perception of reality that she was able to attain. She was perceiving the bliss of being and it was "glorious bliss." She was perceiving our inherent potential.

In the beginning, Jill had no motivation to get to the hospital, but eventually she found a way to reach out to her colleague. He realized what was going on and was able to get Jill to the hospital where she underwent surgery to stop the bleeding in her brain.

Seven years of therapy later, other parts of her left brain took over the functions that had been lost. With the memory of the experience of her right brain, Jill was now able to integrate that reality into her thinking mind. It left her with a richness of first-hand experience that she could now articulate, and she did so in her book *My Stroke of Insight*. Then she summarized it all in her TED talk that later became the most-watched video on YouTube at the time. Twenty-five million views later, she saw this talk transform her life and the lives of many who viewed it. However, in the end, she was very disappointed. Her message that we are all part of a whole and her desire that knowing that we treat one another with a higher degree of respect and kindness seemed to fall on deaf ears. Her encouragement of love and kindness went ignored. But why? Because:

Without the direct experience of the connectedness of everyone in the world, and without experiencing the sheer bliss of being and the flow of Universal Love or Spirit, there simply is no solid basis for people to adopt a different way of relating to others. The experience itself is both the inspiration and the path to a different way of being.

David Hawkins, an enlightened psychiatrist and expert in the development of consciousness, also recognized the importance of the right brain. He writes:

Spiritual endeavor and intention change the brain function and the body's physiology and establish a specific area for spiritual information in the right-brain prefrontal cortex and its concordant etheric (energy) brain. (See: Hawkins, David R., Discovery of the Presence of God: Devotional Nonduality, Hay House INC.)

He talks about how the usual pathway of interpretation—through the left-brain language centers—stimulates the emotional centers in a direct and quick manner, resulting in "triggers" and reactivity. He explains that:

With inner growth and development, the brain changes and the stimulus is processed more in the right brain, resulting instead in greater feelings of peace and harmony, which are a foundation for love.

Our potential is to be making full use of both hemispheres of the brain. Our birthright is to know the bliss of being, know the spirit that informs our life, and live in the awe and joy that is present right here and now. As Albert Einstein said, "There are only two ways to live life. One is as though nothing is a miracle. The other is as though everything is a miracle." Einstein used his whole brain. He saw everything as a miracle. You don't have to be a genius like Einstein. You don't have to be enlightened like David Hawkins. You don't have to have a stroke like Jill Bolte Taylor. You can learn how to have the direct experience of the peace, bliss, and oneness that your heart is capable of.

In order to learn how we can unfold our capacity for living a life infused with bliss and full of awe and joy, we need to know a bit more about how the brain works. Because awakening the heart is not simply about beliefs; it is about the tool through which we perceive reality—the tool that can help us uncover the Light and Love within our own heart.

Your Amazing Brain

The first thing to understand about the brain is that we have, in essence, two different brains in one. Each one perceives reality quite differently because different functions are located in each (half of the) brain. While what follows is a simplified model of brain structure and function, it serves well to help understand inner growth and development and what using our full potential actually means. So apologies to the neuroscientists.

The left brain is where language functions reside. We use language to think conceptually. Our self-concept, our thoughts about ourselves, what we might call ego resides here. How would you describe yourself without using language? Yet you still exist without language, don't you? Think of the ego as those mental-emotional patterns and concepts that are driven by our survival fears and instincts. The ego, in essence, is the personality on adrenaline. It is what happens to our natural personality when we add the fear that something needs to happen for our survival. This patterning is mainly language and concept-bound and thus is processed predominantly in the left brain.

The perception of time is a function of left-brain processing. So our thinking can take us out of the present, and we can look at the past and strategize about the future. We can notice the fine details with the left brain. From these fine details we can create concepts of reality. The left-brain function provides concepts of reality. Thus, we can live in our concept of our past experience and predict future experience, which the ego loves to do. This is why Jill Bolte Taylor describes losing thirty years of emotional baggage the moment her stroke occurred. With her left-brain functioning offline, her past complexes were no longer there.

The ego is survival-oriented. It uses strategy, reason, and logic to aid its main method of survival—control. The ego's attempt to strategize and get needs met is mainly a result of left-brain activity, as are most attempts to end suffering. Our concepts of the world, of life, and of religion all get processed in the left brain. Our understandings of reality from the left brain are all conceptual because left-brain reality is language-bound. The language of mathematics is also in the left brain. These languages allow us to think in a linear, time-bound manner, and to think analytically and scientifically, which is very useful for survival. But there is more to life than surviving. Much more.

Let's contrast this with the right brain. The right-brain perception of reality is timeless. It is silent. If we label the left brain as more ego-oriented, the right brain would be labeled more spirit-oriented or heart-oriented. These are the functions that become more active and dominant as we "wake up." Right-brain perception of reality allows us to experience what we label as "spiritual" states—inner peace, inner silence, and inner freedom. It also allows for our expression of the Universal Heart.

The right brain allows us to perceive things directly as energy and flow rather than forming concepts about them or logically deducing them. The reality here is directly perceived, intuitive, and subtly sensed. We sense patterns of energy and a broader, holistic vision of things. The right brain processes things as a whole, it is holistic, a dramatically different and direct experience of reality.

The right brain is also where creativity functions reside. Art and music are more right-brain processes—the sound part of music, not the lyrics. Music being processed here helps to explain why simple sounds can be used as mantras for meditation. That intuitive inspiration that the artist has is also processed more in the right brain. Intuitive knowing is a right-brain function and skill. More importantly, it is the subtle sensing of energy that is processed in the right brain.

When we engage in practices like meditation, we may at first experience a few moments of inner peace. As we practice more, the right brain becomes more coherent, and the sense of peace, increasingly pleasant, begins to take on another right-brain quality of perception—bliss. This is why yogis sometimes refer to "bliss consciousness." This all has interconnections with one of the most supreme right-brain functions—Love. Love of all types is perceived more through the right brain.

This is important to understand: Through the refinement and growth of our subtle energy perception, our intuitive capabilities, we can begin to know love, not as an emotion, but rather as an energy, a force, the essence of our spirit or being. We can begin to know Universal Love and how it connects us all. This "knowing" is not intellectual; it is direct perception facilitated by right-brain functioning. This helps us to understand both what we are capable of and how this vision of a life of awe, joy, bliss, and Universal love can be lived.

Many important things in life—love, happiness, bliss, inner peace—what we call heart values, result from the development of the right brain.

This is what we mean by awakening the heart—coming to experience more love, happiness, bliss, inner peace, awe, presence, and joy. Awakening the heart is awakening all of these facets and coming to know the essence of our being.

During the initial stages of Jill Bolte Taylor's stroke, she found such peacefulness and amazing perception of wholeness and being one with everything, that she had no sense of anything being wrong. Everything was patterns of energy and bliss and timelessness. Most of us have had this experience of timelessness and blissful joy when falling in love or in deep states of meditation or devotion, in childbirth, or in athletics with being in the zone or getting the runner's high. Some experience it in flow states. Others when immersed in nature. Again, love is perceived predominantly through right-brain perception, and it contributes to the timeless joy of that experience. Remember the right brain is silent—except for the processing of music. Music and the arts can bring us into that same timeless peace, bliss, joy, and flow.

The Two Ways of Knowing Reality

So here we have the two realities: Our left-brain, ego-dominated concepts of reality, and our right-brain direct experience of the peace, energetic flow, and bliss of being. Each of these is valid. Both are important. Too often our left-brain analysis leads us to undervalue or discount the energetic reality and heart values. We consider them too subjective. They are not. Physicists are discovering the reality of consciousness as a field of energy and intelligence underlying all of creation. You can too, by direct experience, through learning to use your right-brain perceptual skills.

Much of what we value in life at the end of the day is more right-brained in orientation. This is where the feeling of being connected to something greater than ourselves comes from. When we begin to activate this connectedness and the awe, joy, and bliss that give rise to compassion and gratitude, we start to discover the Universal Heart. It is larger than the personal heart, which has more connections to the left brain. We don't usually get to explore the Universal Heart. Instead, our culture is heavily survival, ego, and left-brain oriented. We spend years in an educational system that is left-brain dominant, studying language and mathematics. Our right brains are relatively underutilized and underdeveloped. We lack courses on happiness, creativity, and love. But just as learning to read and write and do mathematics takes training and skills practice, so too does developing and awakening the heart.

Awakening the heart requires developing right-brain functioning and integrating it with the left brain. It is like trying to teach yourself to eat or comb your hair with your non-dominant hand. It takes training and skill, developed over time. For people who are more right-brain dominant, integration is still usually lacking and needs to be learned in order to ground intuitive knowing and creative functioning into the whole of life. Without this integration, they can experience switching between left and right dominance, creating frustration and inner conflict, rather than expanding into the vision of the whole experience.

This is the problem with many approaches to inner growth, spirituality, and awakening the heart—the emphasis becomes solely on the right brain. Inner peace, silence, and bliss become the holy grail. Ascension becomes the goal. What is actually needed is integration. We switch the dominance of the left brain to the right brain. We integrate the wiser, more holistic perception of the right brain into the left-brain functioning. We integrate the bliss of being, the intuitive knowing, and the creativity into our daily lives. We integrate peace, joy, and love into all aspects of our existence.

We need ways to awaken and integrate the heart, so we can think with the heart and love with the mind, which means aligning our thinking to reflect the true nature of ourselves, our Divinity.

When we utilize our full potential, perceiving reality with the profound integration of both hemispheres of our brain, we live with such fullness, such joy, so much love and bliss flowing through us, that everything from our spiritual life to our health changes for the better.

How do we make this vision reality? We need to see through the dilemmas of the mind that stand in the way and then understand the psychology of the awakening heart.

Chapter 2

The Dilemmas of the Mind

Without the owner's manual that describes how life works, how to cultivate the heart, and how to live in flow, we attempt to understand suffering and find ways to cope with it. The movie *Beautiful Boy* with Steve Carell and Timothée Chalamet portrays this in the most poignant way. A scene in the movie shows Chalamet speaking in front of a group as part of his rehab. He talks about having overdosed. After resuscitating him, one of the doctors in the hospital asked him,

"What's your problem?"

"I am a meth addict and an alcoholic."

"No, that's how you're dealing with your problem. Now what's your problem?" replied the doctor.

The character goes on to explain the vast dark void that exists within him and his attempt to escape it at any cost, even if it means his life.

The Distraction Approach

What he seeks—the end to his pain, and release from the fear of the void within—has nothing to do with anything outside of him. This is the tragedy of addiction, the attempt to chase away the pain and emptiness within, not knowing that the temporary high can never succeed in doing that, and not knowing the treasures that lie deep within the heart, just beyond the void. In that sense, we come so close to uncovering the Light and Love that we are. It is what makes addiction so hard. We run up to the edge of the pool and out of fear we don't jump in. Then everything becomes harder and harder in life. Deep suffering occurs as we try to distract ourselves from the void within. If only we knew how to navigate that void.

Those who avoid alcohol and drug addiction often try to find distraction through relationships. Trying to find the perfect relationship or make our primary relationship meet the need for excitement and distraction puts undue pressure on the relationship, which can lead to resentment or even the end of the relationship.

Distraction can play out in endless other forms and patterns of addiction from the workaholic to the video-game addict, the shopaholic, "phone glue," researching conspiracy theories, constant attention to politics, and more.

When we try to counter the root of the distraction approach, it can give rise to pursuing "nonattachment." This philosophy has at its basis the assumption that the root problem is attachment to desire. This creates the following dilemma: either I suppress or dissociate from desire and have to face the pain, frustration, and the void within, OR I have to experience addiction, suffering the effects of a harmful substance or behavior, in a never-ending, unfulfilling quest for the next "hit" or "high." That is being trapped by desire.

Here is where people too often go about trying to lift themselves up by their bootstraps. They fall prey to a fallacy of the mind that mistakes the end for the means. "If nonattachment is the end, then I will use my will to be unattached to any desire." This creates a strong identification with the me that is using my will to achieve the end. We become very attached to this me. That creates its own set of problems and suffering. In particular, it creates a lot of self-deception, where we suppress and repress emotion and end up having it come back to bite us later. It makes us sick or causes us to become fatigued, or it allows us to rationalize immoral and unethical behavior, as the subconscious plays out trying to fulfill desire outside of our awareness. To sum up, mistaking the end for the means simply doesn't work.

Here is where the knowledge of the heart and of Universal Love helps to complement and complete the philosophy of nonattachment. When we access awe, bliss, Light, and Love through the tool of the right brain, we come to experience a fullness of heart. From this inner fullness, desire is like added frosting on the cake. We can take it or leave it. We don't have to suppress desire. We don't have to be attached to it. We don't have to go on an endless search to fulfill it time and time again. We see through the illusion that more and more frosting will make the cake taste better. We become unattached to extra frosting by a different means—through the fullness of the "cake" within—through the fullness of the heart.

Awakening the heart allows us to step off the rollercoaster of addiction, out of the binding influence of desire where the only hope of happiness is getting the next thing that we want. Awakening the heart allows us to see that the search outside of ourselves is part of the problem of the missing owner's manual, which is inside us.

The Suffering is Good Approach

This is a popular approach. It goes by many names: The karma clearing approach or the purification approach or the finding meaning approach. "If we glorify suffering, then perhaps we can trick the mind into believing that something good is happening and we won't suffer." Not to say there is no benefit to trying to think positively about things. Not to say either that there aren't times people do an amazing job of finding deeper meaning in their lives and can let go of the past or use the past for good in the future. Still, it does not serve to pretend that something horrible is making us a better person.

The problem is that as long as we are running the ego-based thoughts through the typical left-brain connection to the emotional centers of the brain, we don't really change anything much. Our subconscious doesn't believe a word we're saying when we say, "suffering is good for you—it builds character." The subconscious is more influenced by the experience, and suffering is an incredibly painful experience. So your subconscious doesn't believe you. And it can come back to bite you later with fatigue, illness, or self-sabotage. The dilemma here is whether to try to convince yourself that suffering is good, so you can tolerate it, or go into intolerable pain and suffering. Neither approach solves the problem.

A variation of this approach is often taken up by those who believe in karma and thus see the suffering as getting rid of or clearing "bad" karma. This approach ignores the fact that karma can be transformed. The greatest transformer of karma is Universal Love. When we access that, we can resolve karma without having to suffer through and endure it. This power of the heart to transform karma is little understood, let alone having a clear owner's manual section dedicated to it. Awakening the heart changes the rules of the game and transforms everything.

The Dark Night of the Soul can be part of this suffering-is-good approach when it is extended to purification. We can fall into endless attempts to purify ourselves in order to "ascend." When we have purified and released all the impressions of this lifetime, then we can go on to past lifetimes. It can become endless. Growth and transformation do involve purification, but this need only be to the extent required to clear the way for the Light and Love of the Universal Heart to shine through. Once that happens and we learn how to integrate, the impurities can fall away spontaneously of their own accord. Awakening the heart makes the Dark Night more of a foggy London day. We simply don't need to revel in chaos and suffering and justify it as the Dark Night of the Soul. Here again, awakening the heart and integrating that awareness, as we will explore in further chapters, can greatly ameliorate any suffering that comes with transformation and inner growth, as we anchor ourselves in compassion and self-compassion through our growth and change.

The Monk Approach

And then there's the story of the monk who became a gardener, but soon learned that even in the garden he had to weed out attachments... Many people are drawn to the fantasy of living a monk's or nun's life. Too often it seems like the world is too complex and harsh, full of cruelty and temptations. Going to a monastery, in concept, seems to make the problems go away. Asceticism is held to be noble. However, this is rarely in alignment with the life plan of the individual, and trying to suppress desire either makes it stand out even more, making it harder to control (think of all the spiritual teachers who have been involved in sex scandals,) or it detracts from the life force causing low-energy and health issues. Why? Because the energy of desire contains the energy of the life force. So the dilemma becomes: "Either I stay in the world and suffer or I try to escape the suffering by going to a monastery, ashram, or nunnery only to discover that all my problems come with me."

In the Bhagavad Gita, Krishna speaks of two paths—the path of renunciation and the path of action. Arjuna asks him to say, definitely, which is the superior of the two. Krishna says the path of action. Because the knowledge and awareness gained from meditation must be integrated. That happens much more quickly when we are in the world. Awakening the heart and then taking the awe, joy, bliss, and love that arises naturally in that process, as a foundation for spiritual practices, such as compassion, gratitude, appreciation, forgiveness, and acceptance, rapidly accelerates integration and inner growth. This all has the side-effect (more accurately, side-benefit) of taking us out of suffering in the midst of our busy lives.

The Ascension Approach

The ascension approach is a way to escape the struggles of life by raising our vibration. It is an attempt to maintain a higher state of consciousness to avoid all the Earthly problems and struggles. Raising our vibration and holding a higher level of consciousness and greater awareness—these are great things; however, the dilemma becomes one of how to live in the world and function well if we are trying to avoid the struggles of life. So either we give up on our worldly existence and try to live a transcendental one, or we are stuck with the suffering and pain. The problem comes in that the goal of life is not to get out of it. The blueprint for an individual's life rarely is to just jump out of worldly life. The attempts to do so can result in what is called spiritual bypassing. This is where we ignore or suppress the mental-emotional patterns in favor of living as if we were above things like anger and desire. These unconscious patterns, called "the shadow" in Jungian psychology, often cause us to self-sabotage or engage in behavior that is illegal or immoral, while maintaining a sense that we are really above it all or that it doesn't matter in our unattached, "enlightened" state. This is obviously a prescription for disaster.

Heart-centered living is in complete contrast to spiritual bypassing because it is all about coming to presence and being fully present to whatever arises, whether it is coming from the mind or emotions. It is about integrating the higher vibration into Earthly life; not trying to transcend it. We uplift the human parts of ourselves. We bring Love and Light to all aspects of our existence. We make the subconscious conscious and integrate the deepest compassion, the most profound acceptance, the greatest intuitive insight, and the greatest joy into our mental-emotional functioning. That is what heart-centered living means.

The Religious Approach

For some, religion can be a great salve for suffering. All of the major religions have a mystical sect that focuses on the direct experience of Divinity and Universal Love. "The business and method of mysticism is love," writes one of the world's foremost authorities on mysticism, Evelyn Underhill. Every religion teaches love. But as I shared in the beginning of this book, when I sat there as a young man in the church service and listened to the scripture on Love, I did not understand that what was being taught needed to be supplemented with growth and experience, in order to truly hear and understand the teaching at a deep level.

Too often, the dilemma presented by religions is to suspend your own experience and intellectual understanding and logic, and "just believe," or, "throw the baby out with the bathwater," and turn away from religion altogether, and just accept suffering as part of life. There's a third choice though. It has to do with the direct mystical experience of the truths pointed to in the major religions. It is to directly awaken the heart so that Universal Love flows and one's relationship to all that is sacred and Divine is enlivened. That is something we are hard-wired for. Take a look at Eugene d'Aquili and Andrew Newberg's book titled Why God Won't Go Away, Brain Science and the Biology of Belief. Here is what they say:

"Are the transcendent visions and insights of the great religious mystics based on mental or emotional delusions, or are they the result of coherent sensory perceptions shaped by the proper neurological functioning of sound, healthy minds?

We'll show that the profound spiritual experiences described by saints and mystics of every religion, and in every period of time, can also be attributed to the brain's activity that gives ritual its transcendent powers. We'll also show how the mind's need to understand these experiences can provide a biological origin for specific religious beliefs." Newberg M.D., Andrew; Eugene G. d'Aquili; Vince Rause. Why God Won't Go Away, Ballantine Books, Kindle Edition.

What d'Aquili and Newberg are suggesting is that we are hardwired to experience the mystical, the transcendent, and the subtle energy that is the fabric of the Universe. As we develop the right-brain intuitive perception, we begin to sense and experience the essential quality of this underlying ground of being, which is Universal Love. And this is why awakening the heart is so important. To all these dilemmas there is a solution—we can learn the heart-based skills that use more of our potential and that can create a life of ease and grace.

Chapter 3

Expanding Awareness & The Fullness of the Heart

"Put the mind in the heart..."
— *From the Philokalia (Eastern Orthodox text)*

On March 18, 1958, Thomas Merton was running errands in downtown Louisville when he had an experience that would change his life and influence countless others. The spot is marked with a historical marker to commemorate the mystical experience. It is at 4th and Walnut in Louisville.

Merton described it this way in Conjectures of a Guilty Bystander:

"In Louisville, at the corner of Fourth and Walnut, in the center of the shopping district, I was suddenly overwhelmed with the realization that I loved all those people, that they were mine and I theirs, that we could not be alien to one another even though we were total strangers. It was like waking from a dream of separateness, of spurious self-isolation in a special world, the world

of renunciation and supposed holiness... This sense of liberation from an illusory difference was such a relief and such a joy to me that I almost laughed out loud... I have the immense joy of being man, a member of a race in which God Himself became incarnate. As if the sorrows and stupidities of the human condition could overwhelm me, now I realize what we all are. And if only everybody could realize this! But it cannot be explained. There is no way of telling people that they are all walking around shining like the sun."

Waking from the dream of separateness is that transformation that the mystical brings to a greater awareness of reality. This is the power of awe—it connects us. It brings us into awareness of the fact that we are in essence nonmaterial and in no way isolated. It brings to awareness the interconnectedness of all living beings. And it is transformative.

This is the power of right-brain development. It transforms and uplifts us and creates a new relationship between us and other living beings, and ultimately a new relationship with Universal Love. With that transformation, we see everything as it is, directly perceived as the sacredness that is creation and everyone and everything in it.

Both Jill Bolte Taylor and Thomas Merton were gifted with an experience of what is possible when we awaken the heart. With that wakefulness, we perceive the spirit and energy through the tool of the right brain. Yet, both were challenged as to how to help others easily come to share in what they had experienced.

In order to share in what they experienced, we need to understand how expanding awareness works. So hold onto your hat, we're going to take a fast tour of inner space.

Consciousness—The Basics

Humans are multidimensional beings commonly understood as consisting of mind, body, emotions, and Spirit. We exist on several dimensions. The common concept, however, organizes a person like a pie chart. It is just not what is. This is not the reality that physics and mystics alike have discovered. Spirit, mind, and body are realities that arise from different frequencies of consciousness. Consciousness is a field that underlies all of creation. Like any field, it can vibrate at different frequencies.

The physical level of reality is the lowest frequency of consciousness and feels the most solid because of its density. The next level of reality is the energetic or etheric level. This is the level where acupuncture works, where the pranic flows of yoga operate, and where energy healing works. For clarity, this level of consciousness is best thought of as the vitality level (not just anything nonphysical). It is the energy that informs the physical with vitality.

The next level is the emotional reality. This level has great importance in that how we feel about something makes up a great deal of our experience. Emotions come in all flavors, and as we grow in awareness, we can increasingly describe shades of differences in the color of emotion—like the difference between melancholy and sadness. This emotional level or plane of existence is the level we typically enter into when dreaming at night.

Next is the mental level, the level of thought and concepts. Then is the causal level or the intuitive level or what some call the archetypal level. This is where the archetype for the personality exists and where we tap into for creative and brilliant intuitions or "downloads." It is also where the blueprint for each life resides.

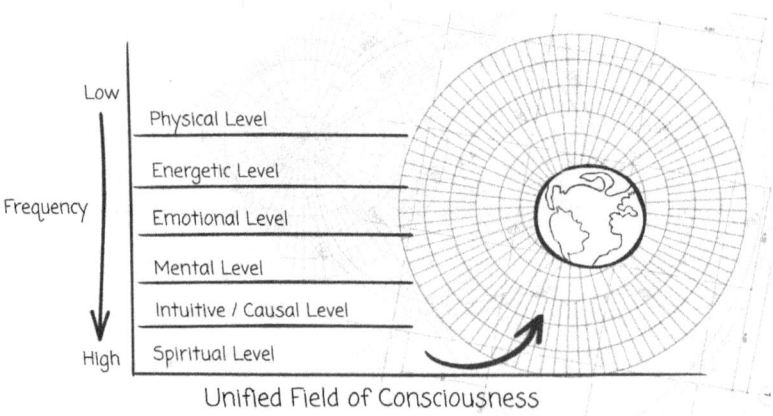

Unified Field of Consciousness

The highest frequency level is the spiritual reality. It is also the level where the Cosmic architecture exists, from which all creation flows into existence. It is the level of Light and Love. The essence of the spiritual level is the blissful energy of Higher Love or Universal Love. Finally, the Unified Field is the infinite frequency of consciousness or Absolute frequency. It is often referred to as pure consciousness or the Absolute.

If we think of human awareness as a telescope, normally we are aiming the telescope at the mental-emotional region. Our left-brain thinking, analysis, and processing of emotions keep us in identification with the mental-emotional constructs of the ego. It keeps the scope looking at those levels of life, perceiving reality through the left brain. This means we are missing out on much of life and what causes and underlies many of the events that take place. Our awareness range or where it is pointing is shown in the following diagram:

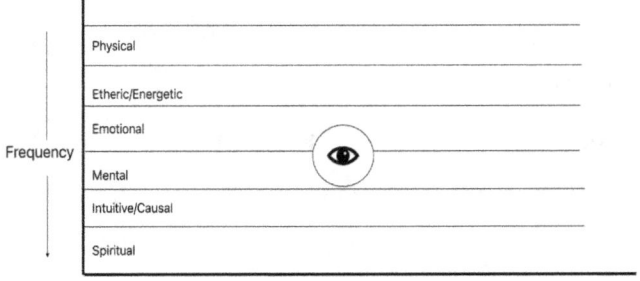

Unified Field / Pure Consciousness / Absolute

So for the majority of people, the telescope of awareness is centered on the mental-emotional planes. Vibrations that are lower than that, we can shift the telescope to. For example, at this moment you probably have little or no awareness of your left foot. Now that this has been pointed out, you have probably shifted the telescope there and are now aware of the sensations.

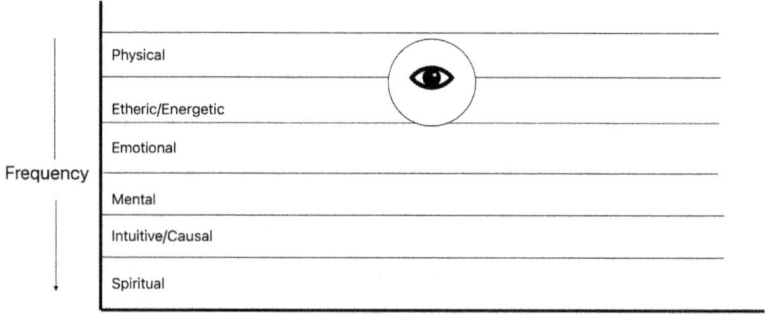

For some who seem to have more functioning of the right brain, they have a whole-body awareness. I remember talking with one of my ballroom dance teachers who pointed out that my core was not engaged and my left knee was outside of my foot. I told her how it seemed difficult to be aware of the music, the steps, holding my arms and elbows up in frame, my feet, and my core all at once. It occurred to me to ask her if she was aware of all of her body at once when she moved. She replied, "Yes, most of the time." I was amazed and impressed. Spatial orientation and music are both mainly processed in the right brain.

In a similar fashion, a psychic can shift the telescope of awareness to the intuitive-causal level of life. They have more facility with the right-brain processing that is involved. However, this is very different from expanding the scope of awareness itself. A psychic hasn't necessarily expanded their consciousness—although they will have raised their frequency of consciousness temporarily by becoming skilled at pointing to a higher level of reality, they may not have integrated that level of awareness or right-brain perception into their everyday life because they are switching the awareness to a higher plane rather than expanding the awareness or using their whole brain.

With our awareness we can perceive through the mental-emotional fields or through the intuitive-spiritual fields. We can use the tool of the left brain or of the right brain. The point is, though, to grow awareness—to enlarge the telescope of awareness to perceive all layers simultaneously. This is an important concept to grasp—there is a difference between shifting awareness to something we haven't seen or paid attention to and actually expanding our awareness.

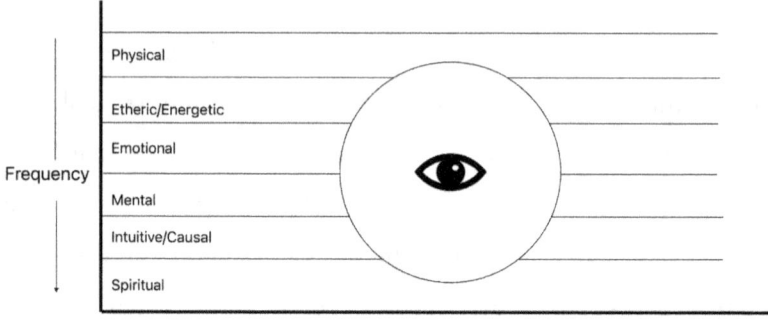

Unified Field / Pure Consciousness / Absolute

If we want to expand awareness, it requires us to be aware of and present to all the levels of our being simultaneously. That means integrating the functioning of the right and left brain in a highly coherent fashion. Initially, it can seem like we have two telescopes or binoculars, one for the left brain and one for the right. What is needed is to see with both telescopes simultaneously, not just alternate back and forth between each one. The heart-awakening practices we will learn in the next chapters allow us to shift awareness to the silent, energy-sensing abilities of the right brain and to integrate that awareness with the left brain. We can then start to maintain awareness of the intuitive and spiritual levels, while we operate simultaneously on the mental and emotional levels. We bring the experience of the peace from the heart centering practice back into our usual life. We integrate the awareness of the bliss of the heart with left-brain thinking and functioning and with our daily activity.

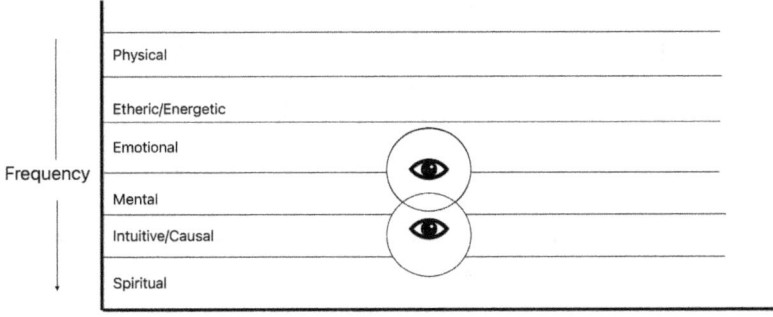

As we work with heart centering—shifting our awareness to the heart space during our daily activities—the two begin to overlap more and more.

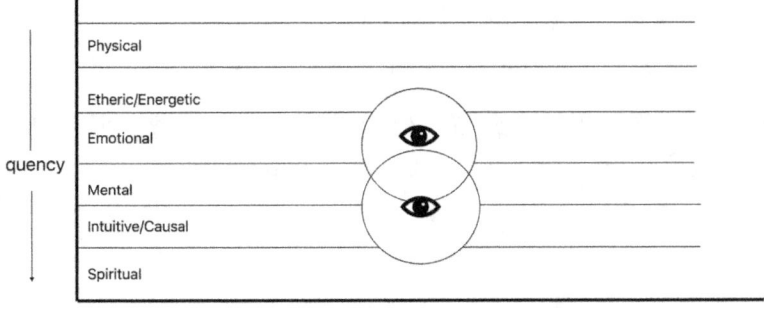

Combined with a deep style of meditation that we will discuss, our perception eventually begins to integrate more fully, with the right brain becoming dominant.

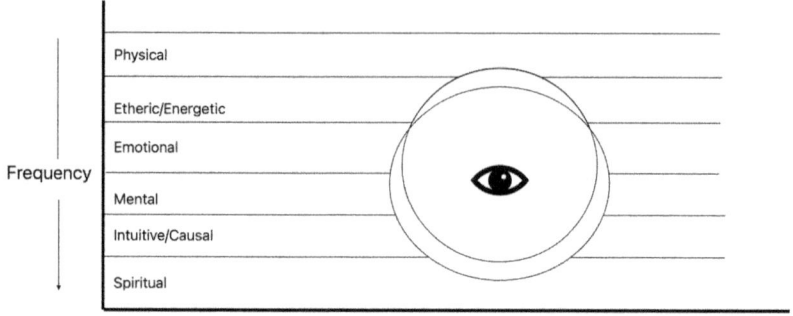

Unified Field / Pure Consciousness / Absolute

Many people miss this point about integration. They attempt to get rid of the left-brain perception and just try to use only the right brain. This gives rise to unintegrated states, often spaced-out states, where we can't function well and go into spiritual bypass (denial of our ego,) and then we miss a lot of the awesomeness and purpose of life—we can miss out on the unique expression of our Divinity and the mission that we came to Earth to fulfill. Thus, expanding, rather than shifting awareness becomes crucial.

Awakening the heart means increasing intuitive and spiritual awareness—we develop the intuitive ability to sense the energies and qualities in the heart space, to know the energetic essence of Universal Love. We then integrate that into our thinking, feelings, and behavior. We learn to think intuitively—to think with the heart. We reorganize the mind to be expressing the Light and Love that we are—we learn to love with the mind. That is the task of growth—learning to think with the heart and love with the mind.

Transcending the Subconscious Programming Traps

Jen was certain of the way out. She had fallen deep into a depression, but she knew it would be temporary. All she needed was to make sure her partner, Jordan, wasn't going to leave her. If she could just secure her relationship, everything would be fine. She wouldn't feel the panic that she was losing Jordan. She wouldn't be depressed if she knew they were okay as a couple. She just needed that certainty. That was all she needed—at least so she thought.

She had come to the psych ward after having expressed suicidal thoughts at hearing that Jordan was unsure if they were going to make it as a couple. He felt smothered and like he couldn't pursue his career without Jen needing to be involved with every step and every decision. Worse than that, he could feel this constant suspicion whenever he mentioned a coworker or a manager at work who was female.

Jen explained that she was certain he was having an affair. She knew she needed help and that she needed to be in a safe place, so that the thoughts of hurting herself did not overwhelm her better judgment. But she also felt like the solution was to be talking to Jordan and making sure he wasn't going to leave.

Her mind was operating in fight-or-flight mode. Everything was black or white. There was white: "If I can only make sure he isn't leaving me, everything will be okay." And then there was black: "If he leaves me, I don't want to live."

With the typical mind, the left-brain dominated mind, the problem is that it is busy organizing everything into categories and evaluating everything in terms of "does it serve me," or "is it what I want" or "is it good." If so, I am attracted to it. I judge it as "good" and beneficial. If not, it is judged as "bad" and I have an aversion to it.

For Jen, trapped in the panic of the left-brain reality, everything was sorted quickly as being for her or against her. When I, as her therapist, listened compassionately to her predicament, I was her best friend. When I suggested that Jordan might need space, I became her enemy and she didn't want to have anything to do with me.

The problem of the mind is that it is typically busy sorting everything in terms of survival—sorting, measuring, evaluating, judging—all means of interpreting reality in terms of survival. Especially judging, as it contains fear within it. We fear some aspect of that which we judge.

The greater problem is this: The mind's filter is perceived by our awareness. **Awareness or consciousness is creative. It moves energy in that direction.** It creates more of that association in the subconscious mind. It gives more energy to that which we are attending to. So in a strange way, we create more of what we fear.

Jen feared Jordan's leaving. Her attempts to check up on him and get reassurance from him had just the opposite effect of pushing him away. When we went over this in one of her sessions, she understood it intellectually. However, her deep subconscious programming and her fear dominated her reality. She just had to know what he was up to.

Even though she had agreed not to call him after our session, she couldn't help herself. Her fear told her that that wasn't really going to help. She rationalized that it didn't matter. She considered me against her and so she went ahead and called him. I saw her on the phone in the hall. She was yelling at him, wondering why he wouldn't answer her questions. Then she yelled at me. "See, I am doing it anyway. I had to call. You can't understand."

Shortly after she was discharged from the hospital, Jordan did leave her. Her fear had created exactly what she was afraid of. She ended up back in the hospital and eventually came to accept that it was over and that suicide was not the way out.

What physicists and sages alike say, is that everything arises out of one underlying field of energy, intelligence, and organizing power. That unified field of consciousness is that out of which all thought arises. It starts outside of the scope of our awareness and arises like a bubble from the bottom of the ocean, getting larger and larger until it "pops" into our awareness. It is just there all of a sudden. So we don't notice it arising, and it can feel like it is our thought because we turn our attention to a topic and the thought is there. What actually happens, though, is that we tune into a channel (a topic) in which this stream of thought is arising.

Every impulse that arises from the unified field of consciousness is a positive impulse of love or creative expression or creative intelligence. It is life-enhancing, life-affirming, life-supportive. Now the problem is that the thought does not pop into awareness in this

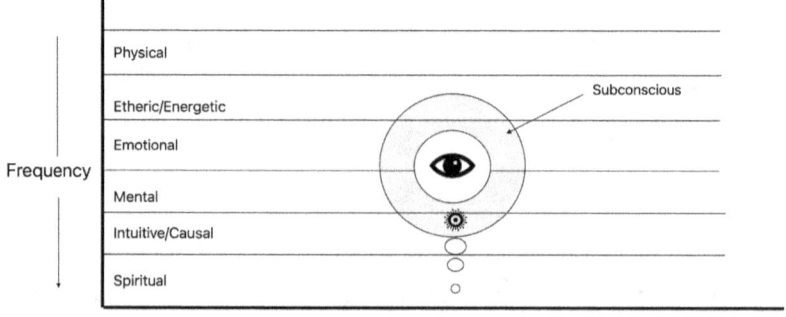

original, pristine form. It gets filtered by the subconscious mind, which contains past associations, mental-emotional complexes, and old programming that distort the impulse before it comes into awareness. It is this distorted version of the impulse that actually comes through to the mind.

If we were to magnify the personal subconscious to show what influences it, it would appear as follows:

As an impulse arises, it gets modified, distorted by the subconscious mind—the accumulated stress, tension, habits, concepts, and past associations. Say a desire for an apple arises—

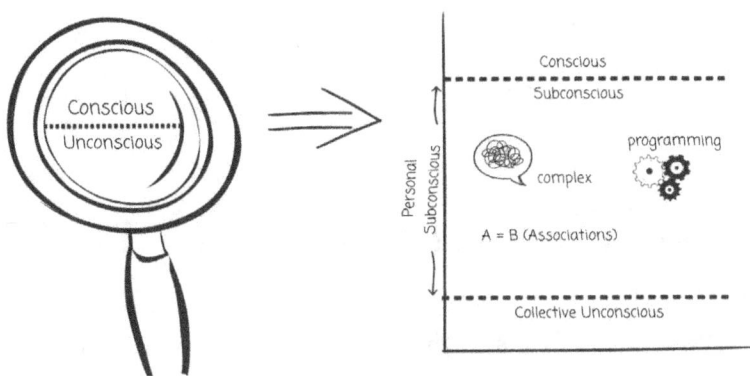

something sweet and light that the body, in its intelligence, is trying to communicate that it needs. As it hits the subconscious mind, the associations with "sweet" morph it into something else. What was a desire for an apple is morphed into a desire for ice-cream.

Say a feeling arises. It is an impulse of awe at the gloriousness of life: "I am glorious life—how amazing I am." The personal subconscious remembers that something bad happened the last time we felt this amazing. It also remembers the childhood training about being egotistical. "I am amazing? I can't say that—that is egotistical. Something bad is going to happen." Out of fear, we turn an impulse of awe into a fear of something bad happening.

Psychologists estimate that 95% of thought is determined by the subconscious mind. That means in order to transform our lives and awaken our hearts, we need to clear the stress, tension, and old programming and associations. More importantly, we need to reprogram the subconscious mind to align with the Light and Love that we are.

Now imagine if instead of receiving every thought through the filters of the subconscious mind, we could create a direct channel from the unified field straight into our consciousness and perceive the original, creative expression of Love that is at the origin of every thought. An awakened heart with an integrated mind is that direct channel. When we practice the heart-awakening technique that we will learn in the next chapter, we bring ourselves into a high vibration. When we integrate that high vibration of Universal Love (through the heart-centering or integration techniques we will cover) into our daily activities, this results in a transformation of the personality and behaviors, which together with our daily activities sit at the levels of the mental-emotional, etheric, and physical. This creates the dissolving effect on the complexes and issues in the subconscious. We take the higher frequency into the space where the lower frequencies (such as fear and judgment) are residing, and in the presence of the highest frequencies of Universal Love, anything lower will dissolve into the higher, in a loving, energetic embrace.

Unlike many common approaches to the problems of the subconscious, we start with the direct experience of the energy of the heart that is the foundation of healing. That means we start outside the mind. We start at a higher vibration, at the intuitive or spiritual level. We start with the right-brain perception of love, and we then make sure we integrate that into the other levels, which makes all the difference. We are not entangling ourselves in our own webs of complexes, but bringing in the healing light to dissolve these.

So we are not using the mind to try to feel something or behave the way we "should." We are using the direct perception of some aspect of Universal Love and bringing this forward into conscious awareness and into our lives. When the heart awakening and integration techniques are done repeatedly, that changes the subconscious mind through the direct channel of our conscious awareness. Remember that awareness is creative. The practices naturally remove a lot of the energy we were pouring into maintaining the old programming and associations. The light of this channel causes the energy held in the old patterns to be released and they just simply tend to fall away.

Our raised consciousness or awareness also allows us to see more clearly when the flow of Love is being hijacked by the subconscious mind. We catch that earlier and earlier, and we are able to respond to that with the natural impulses of forgiveness, radical acceptance, unconditional love, and so on, that arise naturally (as the facets of the awakening heart,) and our experience becomes more and more one of the flow of love. We live in the blissfulness of that flow. This is how we grow.

In Jen's case, she did not have a way out of the mind. She did not have this direct channel, which puts the right brain in the driver's seat and would have allowed her to step back and accept what was happening and give her partner space, which may have saved the relationship. So her subconscious, in the driver's seat, drove her to act in ways that she intellectually knew would not work. The subconscious is or has a mind of its own, so to speak, however, the frequencies of Universal Love that can be brought into all levels of our reality through the right-brain experience and integration, hold the power to dissolve the subconscious problems that are otherwise difficult to tackle. That frees up tremendous energy—we are more lively, more in love with life, and more present in our relationships.

The Psychology of the Fullness of the Awakening Heart Changes Everything

As we engage in the awakening of the heart practices, we shift into a psychology of fulfillment. This fullness of the heart profoundly changes our relationship with desire, our needs, other people, and ultimately with our happiness. A full heart creates a transformation in the experience of life. It heals and uplifts us. It transforms the subconscious mind. Awakening the heart creates a psychology based on Light and Love, rather than on analyzing the darkness. The power of this psychology of fulfillment is best understood with an analogy adapted from one of my teachers.

Imagine you are walking home after just losing your job, you were sacked with no notice. You stop at the bank and take out the last of your money to pay your rent and buy some groceries. You're thinking about how after that, all you will have is a few dollars in your purse or wallet. As you're walking down the street, someone comes running up from behind you and steals your purse or wallet, and all of the last of your money is gone. This is a hugely stressful event for you. Your life has changed. You are dramatically impacted. You don't even know how you will find your next meal, let alone where you will live if you don't pay your rent. How do you feel?

Now imagine, instead, that you are a billionaire. On this particular day you are walking down the street with your personal assistant, and your purse or wallet, also full of money, is stolen. This is the exact same event—the same reality as before. But this time you are not affected. You have so much money in the bank, so many resources, and so much reserve that it is just a minor inconvenience. You have your personal assistant get another wallet or purse, stop at the bank and get some money, and you go on with your day. It doesn't impact you. You don't go into survival mode. You deal with it efficiently and effectively and it does not change your inner state.

Why is this? It is the same event. This is because of the reserves and resources that you have. The awakening of the heart practices provide these kinds of reserves and resources, in the deeper nonmaterial sense. The full heart makes what used to be so important, insignificant. It changes how we relate to needs. It changes our perception of the past. It relieves the fears and associations we carry in the emotional body. Our emotional baggage dissolves. It no longer matters. Our awareness is consumed in the present moment and the perceptions of reality brought to us through the right brain. Events don't have to be interpreted through the old survival programming. We can be fully present to them with an awareness of the Light and Love we carry within us. With that, everything is transformed.

The presence of Universal Love, the presence of the Light within us and outside of us is the awareness we start to carry through the day. Over time, we begin to identify more and more with the Light and Love and less and less with the ego and the subconscious programming. With that, we begin to have a totally different sense of self. That means that the psychology of the awakening heart creates a shift in identity that transforms our inner experience of all aspects of life. This shift in identity greatly aids our inner growth and development. It is this shift that is the hallmark of inner development.

The psychology of the awakening heart allows us to be more present and aware of what is. When we direct attention to the heart space and create that channel in the mind, that is a (conscious) pattern that creates more of that aspect of Universal Love in one's life. Awareness is creative. For example, as I come to know the inner peace and radical acceptance that flow as natural facets of the heart, I begin embracing all that is and can begin to truly love what arises. If someone, say a politician, is demonstrating dishonest behavior, I can become fascinated to see how he will grow and learn to be honest. I can become excited about the growth yet to come. Notice, this is not ignoring the bad or pretending it does not exist—this is being so present to it, that it becomes a fascination. I truly can love what arises without judgment and without becoming energetically tied to the dishonesty that is taking place (if I resist this energy, I effectively engage with it and entangle myself in that energy of dishonesty). With radical acceptance from an awakened heart, I can see the workings of a higher order and have that sense of certainty that all is well, and I do not have to go into a rage at how despicable this or that politician's behavior is.

So in what may have been a situation where I would judge and feel constricted and outraged at someone getting away with something I perceive as wrong, instead, I am fully aware and present to what is and can radiate love to that person so that they may grow more quickly and can feel fascinated by the workings of the Divine. This is not because I am fighting with my mind to "stay positive." This is a natural result of my awareness being heart centered. That shift in attention changes everything. Key to attention in this understanding is shifting our attention out of the mind and into the subtle sensing, which we will soon explore further with more direct exercises. That puts us into a different mode of internal functioning and internal experience. It allows us to "think with the heart and love with the mind."

This radiance of the heart creates tremendous healing. It uplifts us and those around us. It takes us out of judgment and still allows us to be present and to discern. It takes us out of suffering and allows us to live the fullness of the heart and the bliss of being. As we do this more and more, it becomes more and more our way of being. We outgrow suffering and live our full potential.

Awakening the Facets of the Heart

As we begin to live the psychology of fullness, all of the Facets of the Heart begin to unfold in our lives. Like a diamond with many facets, Universal Love has many aspects that we come to embrace and can consciously cultivate. All the facets are interwoven; develop any one of them, and the others will come along. The Facets of the Heart include:

Radical acceptance, unshakeable faith, loving presence, grace, inner guidance, unconditional joy, true appreciation, gratitude, generosity, radiance healing, total forgiveness, and full compassion.

The later chapters of this book are designed to explore and cultivate some of these aspects of Universal Love. We will dive into those after we begin to awaken more awareness of the heart in the following chapter.

Chapter 4

Awakening the Heart

"I have, by persistent practice, learned to drop my attention from the head to a point under the heart. This is separating the I AM from the personal, or limited consciousness, and connecting it with the universal, or spiritual consciousness, with which it forms a union at the point mentioned."

— Charles Fillmore, Founder of the Unity Church in the book Talks on Truth

The challenge to awakening the heart has been to provide a way to the direct experience of both Love and the source of Love. We have discussed that too often love is thought to be "just a feeling." Nothing could be further from the truth. This is made apparent by St. John who said, "God is love, and he who abides in love abides in God, and God in him… Everyone who loves is born of God and knows God. He who does not love, does not know God, for fundamental workings behind the entire Universe is obscured and reduced to a mere sentiment?

The dilemma we have identified is that we perceive love through the mind and the ego until we develop a way to perceive it through the intuitive, energy-sensing right brain. The left-brain approach says that love is just a feeling. It has all sorts of old emotional baggage around love from childhood, and from lovers later on, that makes us perceive it as "just a feeling," when, in fact, it is interwoven into the very fabric of Spirit and Consciousness itself. It expresses itself as the bliss of being, the pull of evolution, and the freedom of inner peace. The solution we have uncovered to this dilemma is for us to step out of the left-brain perception of love and to perceive love through the right brain. This intuitive, energy-sensing faculty allows us to open to the reality that love is.

The heart space is a portal into the right-brain perception of the essence of our being. We leave behind the ego associations with love and we become present to what can be directly experienced. That changes everything. It opens up potentialities we didn't know we had. It anchors us in the moment. It is the mystical experience of coming to know the true nature of Reality.

The fuller context for the awakening of the heart practices that we will now get into has been given in the previous chapters. This is important, as we might overlook many treasures if we don't know the difference between glass and diamond. As we explore and become familiar with the experience in the heart space, we become familiar with the higher frequencies of consciousness and with

Universal Love. To sense and know this directly, we must use more of the right-brain, intuitive perception. Through this we begin to cultivate greater awareness of and use of the subtle senses.

Heart Space Exploration

In order to orient you experientially, we will start with gross sensing on the physical level. We will then move onto sensing the energetic and emotional levels within the heart space. Then we will go more and more subtle.

Typically when I give this orientation to students, it's done one-on-one or in a small group where I can check on each person's experience and make adjustments, helping them to "look" or subtly sense more accurately what is there. Here I would be suggesting you might be experiencing this or that, as a way of prompting you to look more carefully at your experience; not to give you something you are "supposed to" sense at each level. So honor your experience whatever it is.

This exploration is an observation of the heart space using the subtle senses, especially the subtle feeling sense and the subtle visual sense. We are taking advantage of our ability to sense space. In this moment you can sense or feel into the space to your left, without looking at it. When you do so, you shift from a left-brain thinking about these words to a more right-brain perception of reality. The more intently you observe, the quieter the mind becomes. For many of us, the mind doesn't become silent, rather the thoughts seem more distant and slower. That gives us distance from them.

The intention of the following exploration is two-fold: 1) To refine the ability to sense in a subtle fashion; 2) To come to know the higher levels of our being, particularly the spiritual heart.

Honor Your Experience

Whatever you experience, trust it, and know it is okay. Let go of expectation. We can't center if we are focused on associations and expectations. Instead, we innocently observe. We tune into the subtle senses to explore each level of our existence—each frequency band of consciousness in our multidimensional being—utilizing "feeling into" or "subtle sensing" at each level. Just because we are dealing with the heart space, don't get into expecting this exploration will be all love and bliss. If it is, great. Otherwise, view this as a journey with many steps and potentially much variety. First get comfortable, and take a few slow breaths to relax. Then, listen to the guidance that can be accessed through the scan code below:

Video:

Audio:

Summary

This exploration may seem simple and obvious in concept or to the left brain. Or for some, it may create doubt, you may not be sure of what you are experiencing or whether it is significant. Honor your experience and create a practice out of it and you will observe the expansion in consciousness in your life. Remember that awareness is creative, so developing awareness of this spiritual heart, the Universal Heart, will create harmony in your life.

In this exploration, some may find that they skip levels, going straight into the intuitive or emotional level. This can be beautiful in terms of getting to the deeper levels quickly; however, there is value in spending time sensing each level as this helps us know the different levels of life to expand the "telescope" of our awareness after the meditation, rather than switching our awareness. Of course, having a spiritual mentor or teacher of Heart-based Meditation can help guide you in this subtle landscape and refine your awareness of this subtle experience. Either way, the importance of the direct experience of knowing the spiritual level of our existence is paramount. This exploration is intended to be practiced daily. It is opening our awareness to this level of life that changes everything. It is what being spiritual is based on—knowing our spirit and recognizing the Divinity within us. The joy in discovering the essence of Love is that it leads to knowing reality more fully and becoming free. The joy of exploring the heart space comes in the discovery: "This is always available to me."

Heart Centering Integration

Now that we have explored the heart space and come to know the spiritual heart, we can heart center. Heart centering is a practice that integrates the awareness of Spirit or of Light and Love into our moment-to-moment experience. As we become more familiar with the spiritual level of our existence, we can bring that essence into each moment of our day. This is one of the most important practices in awakening the heart, it is the integration we spoke about earlier.

Go Into the Spiritual Plane

Once again, close your eyes, and without going through each layer, go right to the spiritual level and feel into the pleasantness and liveliness and comfort of the heart space. (Just to note, over time when you practice this, it will give way to more than pleasantness—

it will give way to bliss, which is the essence of Universal Love.) Then open your eyes, very slowly, allowing your awareness to stay in the heart space.

Integrate Into the Physical Plane

Now notice the colors around the room you are in, keeping your awareness in the heart space. You may notice the colors have a vibrancy to them. You may feel like you are seeing things in the room for the first time. It may have a clarity and a freshness that comes when we look from this higher level of our being.

Go Back Into the Spiritual Plane

Once again close your eyes and go directly back to the spaciousness and the pleasantness in the heart space and anchor there. Wait a few seconds. Then go ahead and slowly open your eyes.

Integrate Into Your Activities

Now with your awareness still in the heart space, say out loud, "This is a glorious day."

Notice as you speak, you can speak with your awareness still centered in the heart space. You will also typically notice that your speech is a little bit different—a bit slower, slightly calmer, with a different feel to it. Go ahead and say it once again with your awareness centered in the heart space.

Build Your Heart Centering Practice

This is the Heart Centering Practice. This is what to do periodically throughout the day—bring your awareness to this heart space and to the spiritual level of the heart, and start to learn to operate with your awareness here.

Turning your awareness to the spiritual heart is what Heart Centering is. This fosters greater integration. It is the foundation for greater centeredness and greater awareness of who and what we really are.

To support this practice, do it every half hour or more. You will find it is very pleasant, so there will be little resistance in the mind to doing it. All you need to do is remember. So you can put sticky notes around your living space or set a reminder on the phone or do it at the beginning of every conversation. Do whatever can help you to remember and heart center multiple times a day until it becomes second nature. Then watch your life transform.

Intuitive Heart Centered Contemplation

Perhaps the most powerful process in learning to awaken the heart is intuitive contemplation from within the heart space. The heart space is a gateway to our being. From here we can contrast the direct experience of our being with our thoughts, emotions, and beliefs; we can see through the illusions of the ego. We can bring Light and Love to whatever arises and then observe how it transforms as we see it in the Light. This helps to integrate the direct experience of Light and Love—it is integral to incorporating the essence of our being into our thinking and emoting patterns.

Heart centered contemplation can be useful for discovering more about our inner nature. It can be used for decision-making and knowing our individual path more clearly. It can be used for experiencing more clearly the different levels of our existence. Most importantly, though, it can be used for releasing the subconscious complexes, old associations, and mental-emotional programming that keep us trapped in suffering and self-destructive patterns of behavior.

In this practice we observe from a heart-centered place, the pattern and its energy. Often just attending to the energy of the pattern starts it moving, transforming, and releasing. Heart centering takes us out of resistance to the pattern, which is what causes most of the suffering. It allows us to innocently welcome what is present, so we can see into it and see through it. As we simply observe, the power of awareness starts the transformation process. Then we sit in heart-centered openness to intuitive "downloads" as to what assumptions or beliefs are driving the emotion, energy, or pattern. Sitting with that and being present to that in a way that we shine the Light of awareness and the bliss of being onto it, opens us to both insight and healing.

Often an insight comes that allows us to see through the illusion. We contrast the reality of our being in the heart space with the assumption the mind is making about ourselves, for example. Then we see the truth of our existence. This is perhaps best understood through an example.

A client of mine, whom we will call Suzanne, had recurrent challenges to her self-esteem. Her sense of herself was often determined by how pleased her partner, friends, and parents were with her. This was quite challenging because she also had a strong creative drive and wanted to go her own way with her art. The more she would pour herself into her painting, the more anxious she would get. She hated depending on her partner for money. She always felt she was letting him down whenever she would ask for money. This wasn't a problem for him. He enjoyed showing his love by supporting her and giving to her. But she felt obligated to do more for the household expenses.

Suzanne felt like she couldn't feel good about herself because she felt her art was not approved of by others. When she began meditating, she immediately felt less anxiety about all of this, but the challenge didn't go away. She still struggled to feel okay about herself. That is when she sought out my help.

Suzanne had learned to heart center as part of her meditation training. As I guided her to anchor in the heart space, I asked her to describe what her experience was beyond the mental-emotional level. She noted a peace and a sense of spaciousness and expansiveness. Within that spaciousness, she noticed a couple of pinpoint areas of light, like twinkling stars, and a warmth and sense of comfort with her awareness anchored there. From there, I asked her to bring to mind this pattern of needing approval, without going into experiencing it, but rather just to be present to it and observe it—particularly the energy of it.

As she did so, I asked Suzanne to describe the energy of the pattern and where it was located in the body, if at all. She began to describe a red, hot energy with a black center in the region of her solar plexus. Its energy seemed to have pointed spikes, which felt to her like flashes of temper and criticism. As she looked at this from the place of peace and warmth, she noticed it starting to soften a bit in intensity. As it moved and softened, I asked her to open to receiving an insight into this. Almost immediately, she said, "It is saying that I am no good and I have to get others to like me. It's the only way out."

I asked her to sit with that and just look at that assumption and compare it to her experience of herself in the heart space—compare it to the peace and warmth of her being. As she did, she started to laugh. "That is so silly. I don't need others to like me to know I am good. I am goodness itself in this moment, while I am centered here."

"So, you don't need others' approval to know you are good, then?" I asked.

"No. That is just a silly waste of time and energy," she said.

I then asked her to visualize asking her partner for money and to see what would happen now that she had seen through the illusion. Again, she started to laugh. "He is so happy to be helping me out. I don't know why I couldn't see that. It is a joy. It has nothing to do with me or my sense of self."

Just to make sure she had really gotten it, I asked, "Is that really true?"

Her response came quickly, "Absolutely."

"Well done!" I said, and I asked her how her life would be different going forward now. She went on for several minutes like a fifty-pound weight had been lifted off her shoulders.

This is the power of heart centered contemplation to help us integrate the gains of meditation and begin to live a more authentic life. This is how it helps us to release the subconscious patterns that keep us from living our potential. This is a method that greatly accelerates inner growth and development.

The release of the energy is done through the power of awareness and the power of love. Sending our loving attention to the area of the body allows the energy to soften and release. It is the nature of consciousness to make things whole. Our consciousness and attention placed on the area causes it to begin to unite with the greater harmony in our energy system. The fragmented energies are dissolved and reunited with Source through the power of consciousness and the power of love.

Heart Centered Affirmations

This is another practice, usually guided, that can be used to assist integration. We have already seen with Suzanne's experience how heart centering allows us to be more adept at reprogramming the subconscious mind. It helps us to relax the left-brain languaging. It helps us step out of the ego and greatly facilitates conscious reprogramming. This is important work, as psychologists estimate that 95 percent of thinking takes place subconsciously. Often people will use mental repetition of a phrase as a way of reprogramming. Affirmations, however, can take a long time to take hold. It can take many repetitions over many days for this to become a natural part of the subconscious mind. Some try to quicken the process by using more emotion with the affirmation.

Those who work extensively with the subconscious mind, such as hypnotherapists, realize the importance of deep relaxation in the process of influencing the subconscious. While they use a hypnotic trance, the combination of heart centering with binaural beat music is a potent combination that relaxes the ego and the conscious mind. In a quieter, more relaxed internal environment, affirmations quickly become established. As we affirm the truth, we create a channel from the source of thought, from the field of pure consciousness, through the subconscious to the conscious mind. Our affirmations quickly start to pop into our minds during our days and become the "default" programming. The positive, life-affirming impulses that arise from the field of pure consciousness no longer get hi-jacked by the old associations and old subconscious programming. As we stop "feeding" the old programming with our energy and awareness, it starts to fade away. We start to spontaneously favor the truth of ourselves as spiritual beings.

Ultimately, cultivating the heart requires an exploration of the heart space through observation and through the subtle feeling sense. Our thinking and attitudes follow, sometimes soon after and sometimes long after we discover what is within us through observing the heart space. This is what has been missing in so many approaches to inner growth. Experience must come first. Then thinking and attitudes can shift easily. When having the direct experience of awe, bliss, and joy, it becomes easy to shift our thinking and attitudes. Without a firm experiential foundation, we struggle, often unsuccessfully.

As we become practiced at heart centering and work on integrating, we begin to "live from the heart." This is profound. As the Eastern Orthodox text, the Philokalia says, "Put the mind in the heart…" When we do so, we begin to integrate more fully the experience we have in meditation. More importantly, as we do so, we cultivate an increasing awareness of the spiritual level of life. With further practice, we are able to flow this bliss and light to our body, to our emotions, to our mind, to those around us. We become aware of this bliss and light and its ever-present nature. We become aware of its sacredness. The heart space becomes full.

Here then we have the foundation for knowing the essence of our being. Here we have the direct perception of Universal Love. Here we reside beyond belief, beyond thinking, resting in the direct experience of Universal Love, as we awaken to its Source.

This is awakening the heart.

Chapter 5

The Doors of Perception: Awe at the Miracle of Life

"There are only two ways to live your life. One is as though nothing is a miracle. The other is as though everything is a miracle." —Albert Einstein

In 2013 Anthony was driving on the 405 outside of Los Angeles. He was depressed. At 31 years of age, his life made no sense to him. He had just lost his mother to breast cancer and life seemed pointless—"Why bother, when we just end up dying anyway?" Anthony had friends and work, but none of it seemed to matter. He felt he couldn't make any significant contribution to the world, and he was tired of chasing a career and trying to find money and a girlfriend. It was all too much. At his doctor's recommendation, Anthony had tried antidepressants but felt like they just numbed him out, so he stopped.

Driving down the highway, he was sick of the same old thoughts playing over and over again in his head, so he looked down to start a playlist on his phone, and that's when he missed it. He missed seeing the car two lanes over moving into his right lane. As he searched for the playlist, he wandered into that lane and side-swiped the other car. The adrenaline kicked in and time stopped for a moment as he realized he had hit the car. Then time seemed to go in slow motion as he turned away from the other car and overshot, careening into a car on his left, and then totally losing control, driving into the cement embankment where everything went dark.

He was unconscious and would have no memory of being brought to the hospital. Two days later when he woke up in the ICU, he immediately remembered the accident—the slow motion and then the crash into the cement. He had broken his wrist and suffered a concussion, but was miraculously unscathed otherwise. Immediately, upon remembering the accident, an overwhelming sense of joy took over. Anthony was so amazed and so glad to be alive. His depression was gone. In its place was a sense of inner peace and flow. He had a sense of vitality in his body. He felt this indescribable joy, like a flow of blissful love that seemed to make his thoughts feel distant and unimportant. When he tried to remember his sadness or his grief about his mother, they were just distant memories. They held no substance and seemed far from him. It was difficult for him to explain this to anyone. He thought it was just the result of *the concussion. Yet, when he would remember something negative, the thought seemed in the distance and would just slip away into silence, and his awareness would return to the energy and flow of the bliss within.*

Anthony described this period after his accident as being in his sacred flow. He had a sense that he was the flow of energy and love that seemed to be behind everything and seemed to make the thoughts irrelevant. Gradually, after weeks, the thoughts began to have more of a grip on him and his sacred flow started to recede into the background. But his depression never returned.

How can we understand this? Most likely, the concussion and the blackout shut down the dominance of Anthony's left-brain functioning, and he began to function more from the right-brain sense of identity. This allowed him to easily reject thoughts that tried to take him back into depression. He became aware of the Light and Love within and began to identify more with that. Unfortunately, he did not have any training or assistance in maintaining that identity, and so it began to fade and the old habits of the mind started to return—but not completely. He had a profound awakening that would last forever. His experience changed his life.

Actually experiencing the right-brain perception of reality is the only way to come to know the mystery of Reality, to come to know the miracle of life. This is crucial. In order to have a permanent and real experience of change, like Anthony did, we must base our inner development not on mental concepts, but on the spontaneous change that arises from our direct experience. Fortunately, our wake-up call need not be one of trauma. The purpose of our heart awakening practices is to safely and consciously "drive us out of our mind," as I am fond of saying, and into the heart.

Awakening the heart is not just having an interesting experience; we are actually coming to know the reality of life and beginning to create a true relationship with the Light and Love that is within us and all of creation. Awakening the heart is not adopting a philosophy or belief, forcing an attitude, or tricking the mind into thinking differently; it is about experiencing our own true Self. This experience of our true Self changes everything. With a different sense of self, our perceptions change, our behaviors change, and our quality of life dramatically improves.

If we try to force things by working with the mind and insisting "we should" improve our perception and appreciate the miracle of life, it takes heroic discipline—and for most of us, it simply rings hollow anyway, without a lot of energy or heart behind it. Contrary to popular methods, we don't want to be making a mood of gratitude—we want it to arise from deep within us. When we expand our awareness and explore the heart space, this direct experience allows us to be innocently awestruck, and when this happens, we begin to align with the purpose of creation.

If we want to come to know our true Self, it requires us to take a break from the many distractions of our fast-paced culture, which leave our mind and nervous system overtaxed. We must retreat into silence in order to allow the nervous system to settle enough so that we can open the doors of perception. This concept of the doors of perception is something that William Blake talked about. He said:

"If the doors of perception were cleansed then everything would appear to man as it is—Infinite. For man has closed himself up, till he sees all things through narrow chinks of his cavern."

As we spend more time in the simple, subtle practices of awakening the heart, everything begins to appear to us as it is. Everything becomes uplifting and enriching, and that refines all aspects of our existence, allowing us to love what arises. In this way, awakening the heart transforms our lives. The human nervous system is designed for just this. This is the point of having this jewel of a body—it is designed to facilitate our journey of inner development as we expand our awareness through greater and subtler perception until everything appears to us as it is. The human nervous system is designed for us to develop the subtle feeling sense.

When we use heart centering as an integration technique, then we have a foundation for experiencing the awe and wonder present everywhere around us, but all of this is much clearer when we give the nervous system what it needs. This is why rest and slowing down must be emphasized, it gives the nervous system the chance to sparkle in its beauty. We don't need to strive for what we want. In fact, no striving will get you there sooner. Remember striving is a left-brain projection into the future. What we want exists right now—we just need to be settling into it. If we continue along this route of inner development and give the nervous system what it needs, in time, we do cleanse the doors of perception, and our experience becomes more and more one of wonder and awe.

The repeated experience of awe and flow, of loving life and being fascinated by it, takes our energy and consciousness out of the old ways of perceiving. Just like Anthony's awakening dissolved his depression, the experience of awe from awakening our heart, releases old habits of anxiety and worry, sadness and depression, reclaiming for us the energy that was poured into those. As we regain energy and grow more in awe and fascination, no striving is necessary. Your mind is not going to resist bliss at this point. You may have thoughts about resisting it, but the egoic mind itself is always wanting to go to a place of greater joy, happiness, and blissfulness. That's why it's always seeking, the mind is seeking here and there trying to find something blissful. What we discover is that bliss is not out there, it's *within us.*

The bliss then pulls our awareness and attention into the experience of being awestruck by the miracle of life. We simply don't spend as much time investing our consciousness into other patterns, and so they fall away. Remember that consciousness is creative. It works like watering a garden. But the popular expression, "Where attention goes, energy flows" is incomplete; the fuller understanding is that consciousness is more than energy. It has organizing and manifesting intelligence and power. Consciousness organizes life itself. The less time we spend pouring consciousness into old patterns of negativity, the less power these patterns have over our lives. Self-discipline, trying, and striving are not needed. We simply create the context to experience this bliss of the heart repeatedly, and then we rest in it. We start to love our existence and that then decreases and dissolves our need to seek bliss in unhealthy external ways—from sugary food, recreational drugs, alcohol substances, or unhealthy relationships. Awe becomes our natural way of being.

The power of awe is that it connects us with that playful sacredness that stands behind all of life, joining us spontaneously to something greater than ourselves. When we see a beautiful sunset or a rainbow, we want to share it. Because the energy behind awe is the energy of Unity, Oneness, Divinity, and Sacredness. When we are in that energy, we cannot help but want to connect outside of our limited, egoic self. As we cleanse the doors of perception, we begin to see the reality of the Divine energy behind every moment of awe, not just out in nature, but in the eyes of everyone we meet. This is the result of the refinement of intuition and our capacity to sense energy. When practicing heart centering, we are developing our ability to perceive through the subtle feeling sense.

When we transform the functioning of the nervous system to tone down the dominance of the mundane mind, we give way to the holistic, direct perception of reality. So much of the time we are focused on practicality and pour a tremendous amount of energy into thinking that we are assuring our survival. There is a tendency to get stuck in practical considerations, and we don't see the utter improbability of what is right in front of us. A scientist by the name of Fred Hoyle was very much opposed to the Darwinian notion of the entire Universe and human life evolving in some mechanical way out of a primordial soup—that the Universe was just a random set of events that gave rise to life. The probability of that occurring, says Hoyle, is the probability of a tornado going through a junkyard and creating a 747 airplane. Life isn't just mechanical and random; it is the expression of a greater intelligence.

Creation is known by the most astute physicists to be a fascinating, awe-inspiring miracle. Every aspect of creation contains within it such marvelous mysteries. There is fascination in the fact that gravity exists and we don't just float off the Earth, or that the Earth is moving around the sun and that creates the four seasons. The complexity of what is involved is awe-inspiring, all of it highly improbable and miraculous. While Einstein and some other insightful physicists could perceive the miracle of life in the structure of the Universe, everywhere, poets and artists strive to share the awe they have experienced and the connection to something greater that results. For Rumi, the appreciation that came from his experience of awe manifested as an ever-deepening love of the Divine. Appreciation is an aspect of Universal Love. The result, for Rumi, was a compulsion to love everything, which he describes:

To be under the compulsion of Love is to be free.
Other loveless compulsions are like chains.
Love's compulsion isn't compulsion,
It is union with God—
It is the moon emerging from the clouds, shining.

The great mystic Meister Eckhart says, "If the only prayer you ever say in your entire life is thank you, it will be enough." Why? Because it describes precisely the relationship between the individual and the Universe. The Universe is this amazing, fascinating, awe-inspiring, Divinity-infused creation that we are here to discover. And in my own words:

When I tune into the liveliness and pleasantness within the heart space, the bliss that comes seems to spill over into everything I see. A liveliness and vibrancy exists that makes every color more intense, every taste more exquisite, and a sense of awe pervades everything I perceive. I am in awe of everything. Every experience, every moment becomes fascinating. Awe pervades this moment and makes me appreciate every aspect of life. I appreciate everything, from nature to the complexity of a computer, to the simplicity of a sock. Life becomes full of awe and appreciation.

The psychologist Jonah Paquette in his book *Awestruck: How embracing wonder can make you happier, healthier and more connected* talks about how we have this notion that change and growth take place gradually. The truth is, what has the power to transform are the sudden epiphanies that shift our perspective of ourselves and of life. "Ah-ha" moments. Those lightning bolts that mark in memory those moments when we see reality with startling clarity and experience what is truly important, the sacred in life.

As we build our capacity to perceive reality, we begin to find more and more is absolutely miraculous, and we find greater connection and love. Even in the setting of a romantic relationship, awe is incredibly powerful. When we can become fascinated by another person, and in awe of them, our heart opens. Respect and connection are very important for romantic relationships; part of what allows romance to stay alive is our ability to innocently perceive our partner as this unique expression of the Divine. To be continuously in awe of their beauty and kindness and their soul's light creates love and connection.

Increasingly, research defines the benefits that experiencing a sense of awe can create, notably, a decrease in inflammation, which is the precursor to so many diseases, perhaps even cancer. Just recently, the commonly accepted view of a genetic mutation being a key step in the formation of cancer is being questioned. As cells age in the body they are prone to mutations, so if that were the critical factor, we would all have cancer and not be able to manage it. Today, more evidence is being shown that inflammation creates the formation of tumors; inflammation is the trigger that stimulates old cells that have mutations to begin to multiply. MRI studies of the brain have shown that awe is inherent; certain areas of the brain light up when we are in awe, as if it's something that we are designed for, something healing. Another intriguing area of research confirms that when awe stimulates the brain, it encourages the release of oxytocin, a hormone that makes us feel connected to others.

Through the practice of awakening the heart, we step outside of the mind and we begin to turn on intuition—a foundation for experiencing life differently. Einstein is also famous for saying that the solution to a problem comes by stepping into a different level of consciousness than that of the problem. Stepping outside of the mind and becoming innocently present to what is, in the higher levels of consciousness in which the heart resides, this is the foundation for awe. Then everything is awe-inspiring, everything is potentially fascinating. This is the basis for poetry and the arts. Rumi expresses this:

God spoke into the ear of the rose and made it laugh in full bloom.
He spoke to the stone and made it a ruby.
He whispered to the body, and filled it with spirit.
He sang to the sun, and it became radiant.

If we don't see life for the miracle that it is, we are bound to our "loveless compulsions"—living an isolated, egoic existence that is very much a struggle. Taking a step out of that isolated sense of self and allowing awe to overtake us, the boundaries of isolation begin to fade and are replaced by the realization that we are part of an incredible ocean of beauty, abundance, and support. We are part of an ocean of consciousness and are connected to all the other waves. A higher order is responsible for all the flows and changes within that ocean. We are part of that flow and we are protected. When we can get an understanding of this deep into the bones of our being then doubt and concern disappear. Awakening the heart brings us to this.

When we are able to cultivate the heart and find the fullness within us, we find a Universal connection within our own being, and life is transformed. Our life becomes an expression of the Universal Light and Love, and our perception becomes one of constant bliss, awe, and wonder. Then nothing is left to do but laugh a little bit—particularly at all of the concerns we used to have. You can see this innocent laughter in those who have done the work of inner development. It is a wholesome kind of laughter. You can just feel the innocence in yourself and others, as you begin to perceive the fullness of reality that is ever present.

Some people unlock a little bit of this fascination and awe through psychedelics; however, through awakening the heart practices you can achieve this without the risk of drugs damaging the nervous system. Cultivating the heart and the subtle senses will allow awe to be permanent and not just a flashy experience. It's a matter of developing the right brain and the subtle senses for us to intuitively know and experience what is real. We don't see things differently, as in a distorted view; we are instead beginning to see what is actually there—often for the first time.

That's when we are finally able to perceive reality and start to fulfill what we came here to do. We begin to fulfill our personal mission as we start to enjoy life more and become more engaged, perceiving others more and more deeply.

As we perceive reality, we begin to see each person as they truly are, an expression of Divinity. They are 100% ocean, just as every wave is made up of 100% ocean. While each of us have our preferences, and it can be enjoyable to be playing with our preferences and playing with others, it is transformative when we have that direct perception and recognition that every person is an expression of the Divine. Again, every wave is 100% ocean regardless of what they are acting like or if we like how they are acting. Having that knowledge transforms everything.

From awe comes deep appreciation. This is the foundation for real gratitude. With this appreciation, we are so grateful for life and everything it brings us. We spontaneously foster an attitude of gratitude with the awe and appreciation we bring to each moment. With this we discover the grace of gratitude.

As I become familiar with the heart space as a portal into my being, a bliss begins to be ever present. It fills the background and the silence. The entire spaciousness of the heart begins to fill with this blissfulness. As I put my attention on it, what was subtle becomes intense. I feel like my heart might explode. From this, a fullness fills the heart space, and I am in awe of it and of everything. From this, I feel a tenderness and I feel so very blessed. I feel deep gratitude for life, for the opportunity to share with others, for every moment and everything that has brought me to this moment of fullness. I am so grateful to have this life. I am so grateful for all the blessings of this life. I cannot help but say, "Thank you."

As Meister Eckhart said, "If the only prayer you ever say in your entire life is 'thank you,' it will be enough." Here is a Christian theologian, a mentor of numerous monks and nuns, the man who started the Dominican Order of Priests, who is saying, if you had just one prayer, it is not going to be a set religious prayer from any service. Instead, the prayer that expresses everything is "Thank you." Because gratitude communicates the essence of the heart, which is love, this simple prayer goes way beyond prayer and establishes us in a new relationship to life itself.

Meister Eckhart was doing more than communicating with the power of gratitude. He was also communicating the direct experience of reality—an existence filled with love, centered in flow, and fully aware of Being itself. From this broader perception of reality, Eckhart expressed how this heart-centered life is so precious and special. It effortlessly inspires the greatest gratitude, for being in physical form affords us the great opportunity to experience the entire range of life—from the grossest physical aspects to the highest and most subtle, sacred, spiritual aspects of life.

When we hear such wisdom, it is important to understand the context of the mystic's experience—the context for gratitude and its relationship to grace. What happens as we unfold greater awareness is that we come to a tipping point where we finally know everything is perfect just as it is. We know that each mistake is perfect and we know it would be a mistake to not make some mistakes. We know what each challenge is developing in us. We finally know that everything is grace. In that knowing, we come to the greatest awe, and from that, gratitude flows.

Imagine, for a moment, that you knew deep in your bones that every single thing is for you. Deep in your bones means not just "Well, it's not against me," or "I can just accept it," or "I might be able to bear it if I really try to convince myself there is a silver lining here somewhere." What if you knew in your deepest heart of hearts that everything is arranged for you and your learning? And you knew that it was the absolute best possible thing for you in this very moment—that it was more than okay—it was actually something that you asked for.

As far-fetched as that may seem, imagine what your attitude would be like. What if you could meet every single challenge knowing that it was perfect and arranged exactly for you? How would life be different? How curious would you be about what was going to unfold next? How quick would you be to see how each challenge was helpful in your growth? What if you were so grateful for the challenges that you ran to them rather than running away from them? Wouldn't challenges no longer be seen as challenges? Instead, wouldn't you be thanking yourself for having the opportunity to be transformed by what was present in your life? Would you not be in awe and gratitude for this life?

Every day in the mystic's life on this path of the heart, you end up giving thanks for every aspect of life and for the people and the opportunities in it. And every day you feel that Universal Love, and that connects you to something greater. You feel a sense of perfect synchronicity. You feel Universal Love orchestrating every single event, blessing you with knowledge, growth, and wisdom. What would it be like to live like that? How could you not say thank you to life? How could you not say thank you to Universal Love? How could you not say thank you to the Divine?

This is what is meant by radical gratitude: being grateful for everything—even the things we don't like. To be grateful, not just for the good, but for everything that is brought to us—that is a difficult task for most of us. Integrating death, disease, and struggle into an authentic practice of radical gratitude—that just does not seem possible for most of us. How can I be grateful for a disease that robs me of money and time doing the things I love? On the surface that can seem inauthentic, like trying to trick the mind into thinking that something is simply not real—like trying to trick the mind into thinking that up is really down. "How can I be grateful for something that hurts?"

Take, for example, the death of my brother. It was difficult because it was just totally off my radar. I never thought that my brother would ever pass before me. We were so close in age. At the time he was diagnosed with cancer, I was working with an amazing group of distance healers, and I thought we really had a chance to help him be cured. It was shockingly disappointing that we couldn't. I learned that I can't control things, even with the best intentions and healing techniques. I learned that there is a bigger plan at work. I just accepted it rather than finding any gratitude in it. Years later, I discovered some of the keys that would allow me to come into authentic gratitude.

The first key is to remember you can't trick the mind. We can make this common mistake where we try to use the mind to drag around the heart. We say, "Now come here and be grateful for this." While this is all well-intentioned, grace and gratitude are really about getting beyond the mind.

When we are in the fullness of the heart, nothing stands in the way of the Light of Universal Love. We have an innocence and curiosity about everything that happens. "Oh, I didn't expect that. This is really surprising. I wonder what this is about?" Simultaneously with this innocence, a deep knowingness comes. We know that everything is going to be alright. We know that important gifts are coming, we don't need to chase after them or figure them out. They will become apparent through this experience.

So in the year since my brother's passing, when I'm able to be heart centered and live from that standpoint, I have been given so much. It is not that my experience has been without sadness, but when it comes, it doesn't last long. When I heart center, my experience spontaneously shifts to one of gratitude. I feel a deep appreciation. I give gratitude knowing that I've had a longer life than he did. I am amazed at that and how unexpected that is. I am grateful to have had a brother, grateful for all he shared with me, all the advice he gave me, and the ways we were able to connect in our teenage years. I am grateful also for a different kind of relationship—the deeper relationship I had with him in his last months, which I will forever treasure. As I practice getting out of the mind and my intuition develops more and more, I have a clear sense of him and his life on the other side. This is an amazing blessing for which I am immensely grateful.

It is not that I am trying to be grateful. It is not that I am in that state all the time yet. More and more, though, my daily experience is one of awe and feeling blessed. Gratitude flows frequently. Turning to the fullness of the heart space evokes spontaneous gratitude most of the time.

When we're lingering in gratitude, we're lingering in the fabric of our being, connected to the Universal Heart. Lingering in gratitude taps us into flow. When we are lingering in the flow of Universal energy, it not only revives us, it also harmonizes us. It's the foundation for synchronicities and abundance. To the extent we are grateful for what is, we enter into that flow, which allows us to pull in more abundance, wealth, awe, and beauty. One of the wealthiest investors ever was Sir John Templeton, who had started his life without wealth and became one of the greatest investors of all time. During an interview, he was asked what the secret to wealth is. He answered immediately. "Gratitude. Because if you've got everything and you're not grateful, you're poor. And if you seemingly have nothing but you're grateful for even the littlest things, then you're rich. Money won't make you rich. Only gratitude will." Gratitude puts us into the flow of Universal intelligence and its organizing power. It also raises our vibration and blesses our life. It makes us rich in Spirit. It forms the foundation for us opening to a greater flow.

When we resist what is, we block the flow. We block the flow of life energy and synchronicities when we are in resistance to what is. That is why gratitude becomes so powerful because it can put us back into that flow. It can put us back into that very dynamic, very lively Universal intelligence that organizes everything. The process of heart centering is really about shifting out of the mental habits, judgments, and resistance, and stepping into being. When we take that step, we step onto the escalator. It raises our vibration, and we become in awe of everything that we see around us. We enter into the flow state. It's the transition into the flow state that creates the opening for Grace. We step into the flow of Grace itself.

Too often, the nervous system is too stimulated to be in the flow. Overstimulation is stressful, takes a lot of energy, and puts us into a black-and-white kind of survival thinking. This motivates the mind to attend to the negative. If we are focused on survival, we are looking for those threats to survival. We scan for threats. These are not the threats of living out in the wild; instead, these are threats to our self-esteem, or to our happiness, or our sense of security. When we relax and come into the center of the heart, we shift out of the mind, and this sets us up for the natural expression of gratitude.

It also sets us up for perceiving how awesome every facet of life is. It is an important first step in the art of gratitude to center in the heart because it puts us directly in the flow of the energy of gratitude and into the greater Universal Flow. We can then be fascinated by the simplest thing—something as simple as a pen. Looking at it as if for the first time, we become in awe of how amazing it is. What if I had to build this pen from scratch? What intelligence went into being able to make even this simple thing work? How amazing is that? And how amazing is it that I can just reach out and have this? And what about running water? Think about all that goes into that. Or into a computer. This gratitude and awe for what is becomes the foundation for abundance.

In so many ways, we have mistaken the end for the means. That is why the emphasis on heart centering. This habit cultivates a way of being that results in a new attitude. We are restructuring the personality based on our direct experience of something greater— the fullness of the heart. Advanced souls know this intuitively. But they don't always know how to show others to this place.

When you realize that everything is being brought to you for your learning, growth, and ultimate joy, life transforms. Suffering decreases and joy expands. So gratitude can become a habit or a practice, but it is most effective when it is an outpouring of Universal Love. It flows spontaneously from the recognition of the Divinity that we carry within us and an awareness of the Divinity around us. So don't turn this into work. Let yourself desire to have the experience of living a more heart centered life, living more from the heart space. Then simply fan the flames of that desire and everything will unfold from there.

Chapter 6

The Peace that Passeth Understanding: Radical Acceptance

A magician concludes his act with a final bit of magic. He tells the audience he will give a magic formula to just one of them, a formula that will give them anything they want in life. He asks who is interested. Hundreds of hands shoot up in the air. He asks one person to come up on stage and says, "There is one and only one thing you must do to ensure that you will from this point forward get everything that you want in life. It is a special instruction that you will need to memorize and practice daily. Are you ready to do this going forward?"

"Yes, indeed," comes the reply.

"Here is the instruction: 'Want what you get.' Do this practice daily and you will have everything you want in life."

The search for inner peace can take many approaches. The approach that creates true transformation and integration is one where the shift is based on our inner experience, where our acceptance is based on our inner state rather than on philosophy, thinking, concepts, or magical incantations. When we cultivate the heart and sit intuitively and look at what the Spiritual Heart holds, we open to realization. With that, a shift takes place in our experience of life. When we don't base transformation on experience, then we are just using the mind to try to force itself into changing. We end up chasing ourselves in circles trying to get ourselves to adopt an idea when acceptance is not idea-based. Acceptance is an expression of the heart. Acceptance is an expression of wholeness, which allows life to unfold with deep trust, knowing that it unfolds in a higher order.

Cultivating and experiencing the fullness of the heart allows us to embrace what is. The trick is not to be fooling the mind by saying, "This is like cough syrup, it's going to be good for you. Take it even though it tastes terrible." No. It's not a mental thing. What is required for us to have this profound shift and come into true acceptance has to do with us being able to step outside of the mind. Looking intuitively at the heart space takes us out of concepts and ideas and into direct experience. Doing so, we cultivate the heart.

Cultivating the heart expands our awareness of its qualities and capacities. Cultivation comes through repeated observation, and as the heart's potential grows, unfolds, and is realized, the various illusions that snag the mind and cause us great suffering start to fall away. When we bring in the light, the darkness is automatically dispelled. When we access that field of peace, bliss, and love, it gets quickly integrated into everything that we do.

An expansion of the heart occurs with the practice of heart centering. Over time, this creates a snowball effect—the expansion accelerates and accelerates until the heart can hold everything. We have the fullness of heart to accept anything. Radical acceptance, though, comes when we can embrace everything—when we have the realization that life is for us. But you can't get there from here, as they say in Maine.

To get there, along with expanding our awareness through meditating and stepping out of the mind by exploring the heart space, realization is greatly aided by having curiosity when the heart feels constricted or when the emotions feel unpleasant. We can begin to recognize that as feedback. We come to see constriction as something we are healing, some old belief structure that we are ready to release. Some aspect of our being is calling out for greater love. Something within us is looking to be embraced. To make this a little bit more concrete, I will share a personal story that happened to me recently.

My dear father was in the hospital and I was looking at accepting whatever outcome may be, observing where I would come into feeling a "pinch" in my heart space. I looked at where I would come into feeling a tenderness, where I would come into resisting what was transpiring, or where I would need to know what the outcome was going to be. As I heart centered and stepped back into that Universal Love, I became aware of an aspect of my personality that still holds judgment about suffering. There is still resistance to not being able to do everything that I want to do. I began to see a theme that has been there throughout this life. I had difficulty embracing the suffering, which is the reality for so many people. Acceptance doesn't mean that we like it or don't care about it. Acceptance means that we are not in resistance. We are not out of alignment with the Universal Love and the higher order that is supporting each and every individual's life. I came to understand that my need for real deep acceptance in terms of seeing others suffer, was a calling out for a greater expansion of the heart, opening to a greater ability to love people through whatever they are going through, particularly those people I am closest to.

Since that realization, I have been able to hold my father in whatever outcome would be with the highest love and light. I can just be there for him with this infinite compassion that is the nature of the Universal Heart. Tenderness and caring are still there, but not the angst and the suffering in witnessing what is taking place. Instead, I can just sit in the Love and be present for him on his path.

Again, acceptance doesn't mean that we like it or that we don't care. Acceptance doesn't mean that it doesn't matter. What we are talking about with radical acceptance is growing the heart so big that it can hold anything and realize that it is for our growth, for us, in some profound way. This beautiful heart that each one of us possess is capable of holding the entire world. It is capable of holding all of the suffering and of holding every person on the planet.

As we practice heart centering, deeply exploring the spaciousness within, we discover the causes of constriction. As these come to awareness, if we remain heart centered, we can become free to love whatever arises. The heart center gives us peace that fosters expansive love. Becoming present to what is and being in the experience of peace with what is, we can see that every soul has perfectly organized the exact experiences they have in life. As we grow the heart to be able to love what arises, we can truly come to radical acceptance where we actively embrace and flow love to whatever is. We create a deep and unshakable knowing that every individual is experiencing exactly what is for their highest good.

This is not about believing this is so. This is encouraging you to come to explore and discover this amazing heart that each of us has. This amazing heart can hold space for everything. Once we go beyond the mental-emotional layer of consciousness—once we identify with the Spiritual Heart—we are able to hold our own emotions within that greater heart. We are able to hold our own sadness, worry, and concern within that greater heart, which creates the deepest, most profound healing possible. Radical acceptance is healing that comes through the cultivation of the heart. It is the ability to get beyond resignation and into active appreciation for this amazing life and all that it holds. Many people will say their greatest challenge has also been their greatest gift. To get there, we have to step out of the mind and into the heart and discover the wisdom within every event of life.

As opposed to philosophy, this is a process of deep healing. Typically, we do this healing gradually. To understand the foundation for this healing, we need only look closely at the fundamental experiences that we have within the heart space as we heart center and shift our awareness from the mind to the spaciousness of the heart. The first experience is peace. Exploring the pleasantness of the peace, diving into what it feels like, we take that feeling to its ultimate: bliss. When we go deeper into that, the intensity grows, and we become full of bliss. Going further into that, we come to an experience of oneness with the bliss. The full experience of this unity aspect of the Universal Heart brings about a merging with every other being and everything in the Universe.

In order to deeply know acceptance and to be able to hold everything in the heart, even when it breaks, we need only explore the first of these three fundamental experiences of the heart space—peace. Peace is the foundation for radical acceptance.

The essence of radical acceptance is the ability to embrace and move towards what challenges us, rather than simply capitulating and trying to let go. Even the word surrender can have this connotation of giving up. Raising the white flag says, "I'm done fighting." It is good to be done fighting and resisting, this can be acceptance. Radical acceptance, in contrast, is taking it a step further by coming to meet the challenge and embrace what is happening. To be able to hold in your heart whatever is transpiring requires a shift in your beliefs. A most important shift is created when we take a situation that we are in resistance to and we heart center. We come to peace, let go of the resistance, and sit in the questions, "What if this is for me? What if this is something prompting my growth, greater development, and greater heartfulness?" Sitting in peace with these questions brings us the insight that allows us to embrace the situation and move forward. This moves us to discover the Divinity within each moment, the sacredness within each life event. No doubt some experiences are horrible—but remember that is the mind's evaluation. Our conditioning often blocks our ability to see the sacredness, Divinity, and higher order or bigger purpose.

In order to see the bigger picture, we can remember to heart center and ask this question, "How is this for me?" Even with this, it can still be difficult to come to radical acceptance. Here's how I've come to greater acceptance in my own struggles. I've searched for the deeper meaning in the situation. As random and chaotic as life may seem, a higher order is at play. Finding that higher order allows us to see exactly how this is for us. "How do I find the deeper importance, the deeper purpose in this? How have I arranged for this experience? What is my soul seeking? What is the deeper meaning here?" When we talk with people who have been through really horrendous experiences, those who have come to peace with everything often talk about how important and transformative those experiences were. They often talk about how the horrible experience was a setup for them to discover some hidden potential or strength within themselves, how it helped them to unfold their gifts and make the most meaningful contribution to others' lives.

The greatest challenge can be key to the greatest fulfillment. It unveils something that we were needing to learn. That's certainly the case for some. In the book *Your Soul's Plan, Discovering the Real Meaning of the Life You Planned Before You Were Born*, by Robert Schwartz, a poignant prologue goes like this:

On February 25th, 1969 Christina, a 20-year-old administrative assistant in the Department of Political Science at Pomona College in Clairmont, CA went to the department's basement mailbox to pick up her employer's mail. As she touched a package in the mailbox, a bomb detonated hurling her across the room. Dust and soot filled the air, 6-foot splinters of wood shot like arrows into the cement wall behind her. Flames from the explosion scorched Christina's face leaving her temporarily blind. The blast severed two fingers from her right hand and ruptured both eardrums. Christina planned this experience before she was born, and she knows why.

It is coming to know the "why" and developing the trust that there is a "why" even if we don't know what it is, that allows us to transition from acceptance to radical acceptance. (If you want to know Christina's "why," get the book — it is a fantastic read.) When we sit in the heart space and we intuit, "How is what I am resisting for me?" —then we find a deeper meaning that connects us to our soul's purpose in arranging the events of our lives.

After we have gone through this process of intuiting how these events serve us, several times, then we start to trust. We see how everything is for us. Then we can make it a habit to joyfully embrace each and every challenge, to lean into whatever problem is creating resistance in us. In leaning in and embracing the challenge, we embrace life and come to love it joyously. We live the ultimate truth, which is that life is for us.

But sometimes finding meaning can be too mental for us; the mind jumps in and the process is no longer intuitive. In this case, I focus more on the refinement of perception. As we work with intuition more and we start to sense energy, we start to sense how permeable the physical world is, and we begin to have a feel for the energy that is behind life. We begin to be able to perceive the subtle light that permeates our existence. As though beginning to see or sense the aura around others, we begin to notice that everything in creation has a glow to it and that there is light permeating everything. When we come to somebody who is challenging, instead of seeing their anger, criticism, or their obstinance, we see the light that shines through them. We literally see their Divinity that is being masked by their behavior. In seeing their Divinity, we realize that there is this higher order and that this is an expression of the Divine.

While our emotional body may react and get triggered, over time, as we continue to see the Divinity within every soul, we react less and less. We can see the contradiction and identify more with that person's soul and their Divine being than with their mental-emotional expression. In other words, we identify less with their egoic expression. This subtle ability is something everyone who develops the subtle feeling sense comes to eventually. Perhaps you already have it in meditation; it is only left for you to remind yourself to see it outside of meditation.

However, in time, as you grow your heart to be able to hold and embrace everything, you may not even need to question what the meaning or purpose of life events is.

Ultimately, the practice of radical acceptance expands our heart to lovingly hold whatever is. This is the result over time, regardless of how we come into radical acceptance. We are able to radiate Love and Light to whatever arises because this is easy and natural for the awakened heart. With practice, we become free, stepping out of resistance to what is. We become free from suffering, not through detachment or nonattachment, but through an amazing fulfillment. It doesn't mean that we don't try to change things or don't speak up when someone is being hurtful. It doesn't mean we let go of any sense of right and wrong. All of that becomes anchored in a backdrop of the greatest compassion, joy, bliss, and the ability to love to the extent that we can hold the entire world and all its problems and all its suffering in our heart. Like the mother who soothes the child who has fallen down and skinned his knees, we are able to soothe and help others to heal by the depth and breadth of the Love we hold for them.

Through the practice of radical acceptance, we become transformed. Behind much of the angst, struggle, and all that we can't accept, is an attempt on our part to try to make things happen in the way we think they "should." This is particularly true with the people we are closest to. Not only is that presumptuous but it's also impossible for us to truly know what's best for someone else.

This presumptuousness is portrayed in a scene from one of the outtakes of the movie Bruce Almighty where Jim Carrey is given the job of being God and being "Almighty." At one point, he is walking past a playground and there's a bully beating up another boy. Bruce uses his power as God to give the boy who is being beaten up a super amount of strength, and the boy is able to beat up the bully. Morgan Freeman, who is playing the real God asks, "Why did you do that?"

"Well he was being beaten up and I didn't think that was right." This is when Morgan Freeman explains that it is not right, but asks him what good he has done turning the weak boy into a bully. Freeman points out that the boy's destiny, up until that moment, was to take the pain of being tormented by this bully and use it to write the most beautiful poetry that the world has ever seen and to become a Nobel Prize winning author. Instead, he ends up a bully living a life of repaying grievances. The movie makes the point that sometimes we think we know better than God. We are profoundly humbled when we realize that we don't. We need to let go of that subtle arrogance that puts us into resistance to what is. Expanding the heart, we develop an appreciation for the greater intelligence that has organized everything on this planet. We begin to respect the mystery of life and we let go of the need to understand how it will unfold.

Developing this level of trust is difficult to do. Even when we intellectually recognize it, the emotional body still resists until we can embrace and love both ourselves and others through whatever challenge is being encountered. From that Love, we begin to see the Divinity that each of us is. We begin to see the support that we all have and feel the Love and Light that surrounds each and every human being. We become aware that the moments of "luck" in a person's life are not really coincidences. We begin to see the Light and Love that has guided the person to that moment.

Love carries us into nonresistance and gives us greater life force so that we have more energy to become more, to do more, to give more, and to change more—all from the profoundest state of acceptance. We feel a joy in seeing how each soul is held and is not alone.

The famous parable called "Footprints in the Sand" demonstrates this. It is about a person meeting with God and having his life shown as a journey, walking down the sandy beach. Each step of his life is being mapped out on this beach, and parallel to the person's footprints are another set of footprints. As they are reviewing his life's journey, there is a part where his life is really hard. For this person, the hardest times in life are shown with only one set of footprints, instead of two. The person asks God to explain who the second set of footprints belongs to. The answer comes, "The second set of footprints are mine, I have been with you all along the journey."

The person asks, "Well here, at this most difficult time in my life, the place where I struggled the most, there is just one set of footprints. Where were you when I needed you the most?"

The reply comes—

"That is when I carried you."

Expanding the heart, we eventually know we are loved. We begin to expand into love in response to whatever anyone brings us. If it's joy or appreciation, we love and acknowledge that. If it's anger and criticism, we understand the depth of pain they must be in to need to go there, and we hold them in our heart. We love this opportunity to be able to help them heal by our compassion and to help ourselves heal by sending love to whatever triggered us, so that it may be released. As we do this, we begin to know the peace of the heart, we realize Universal Love is unstoppable. It cannot be destroyed. It can be pushed out of awareness. It can be closed off. But it can never be destroyed. The Universal Love of the Heart is always there in the midst of the peace within. With that, we love whatever arises in the world, knowing that it is so in need of healing and it does not need our criticism and judgment.

We can discern that someone's behavior isn't appropriate. We can discern that this isn't what I want. We can discern that this is not ideal. At the same time, we can have a deep, deep trust. Just like Christina, who came to know why she had planned to pick up a package that was in fact a bomb that would blow her across the room, we can know that each and every soul has planned to be here at this time for this exact experience. We balance what we discern with a heart full of complete peace and compassion. The total honoring of each individual soul naturally arises in us, acknowledging the courage they have in undergoing these experiences. This further inspires us to let go of any fear, any judgment driven by fear, and any resistance to what is. When Love flows to whatever arises—then true happiness is ours.

We can find the joy of service and the joy of creating something better in the world, without having to be angry at the world like I was as a young man. The joy can become our habit as all of the conditioning and everything we have been told about how life is supposed to be and who deserves what, falls away. This is the way of the heart—the way that cultivates true bliss and joy that can't be overshadowed by anything. It is present behind any tears of sadness. It can carry us through any tragedy. It carries us when we no longer have the strength to walk our path and make those footprints in the sand.

Radical Acceptance and True Surrender

In 1952 a physicist by the name of Lester Levenson was sent home by his doctors to die. He was told that he should not take a single unnecessary step as it could risk his life. This was a terrible and shocking situation, as he had always been so active in his life. He was overwhelmed with an intense fear of dying. He realized everything he had been taught about philosophy, psychology, and social science could not help him. But he knew he was intelligent. So he decided to use his intelligence to examine his life. He sat with questions of what the point of his life was and what the point of every life was. What do we all seek? His answer: Happiness. As he examined what made him happy, Lester discovered the connection between happiness and love. He also discovered what stood in the way of both happiness and love.

From that, he realized an important truth that literally saved his life. He realized his own feelings were the cause of all his problems; not the world or the people in it, as he had previously thought. He also realized his own feelings were what he had struggled so hard and long against. And this struggle was what had destroyed his health and caused him to suffer in every way. Lester discovered a way of coming to peace with his feelings and allowing them to be released. He discovered that rather than suppressing them, coping with them, or venting them, another option existed. This became the foundation for the Sedona Method of letting go. An important aspect of this was accepting the feelings. As he worked with this more and more, Lester became healthier and happier and eventually went on to live an exceptional life for another 40 years. In many ways he discovered the essence of radical acceptance.

Radical acceptance incorporates true surrender. When we understand surrender in terms of its ideal foundation, then everything changes. We discover that surrender is much more than simply letting go. Letting go, we have the chance to pick it up again; with surrender, we give it over entirely. We no longer "own" it. We are no longer defined by it. All of that implies that a true healing process takes place. Whatever motivation we had to be hanging on, to be identifying with, and to be involved with, ceases. Why? Because we step into something greater. Three distinctions are important here. First, surrender and letting go are quite different. Second, surrender and giving up are also two very different things. Third, surrender is an aspect of radical acceptance.

For too many, surrender has an association with waving "the white flag," which implies defeat or at best a truce. True surrender takes us into an unfathomable joy. It takes us into the bliss of our being. So it makes a huge difference when we move past the concept of surrender as a release and instead ask the question, "What are we surrendering to?" Even this does not describe the context properly because it implies some external force. A more accurate question would be, "What are we surrendering into?" When we have the foundational explorations of the heart space, then this becomes clear and surrendering becomes a joy. The same inner peace that forms the foundation for radical acceptance promotes true surrender.

The real joy in surrender comes when we discover that the most efficient way of true surrender is surrendering into something blissful within ourselves. It is very difficult to be focused on "not something" such as "I want to surrender my anger, so I am focused on 'not being angry.' I want to not be consumed with anger." This is a tall order, like trying not to think can make meditation very difficult. It's the analogy of trying not to think of a giraffe; the more you try, the more you fail and the more you see giraffes everywhere.

In meditation, we are letting go into our being. Being's nature is peaceful, blissful, and has an essence that is joyful. Therefore, we are surrendering into something. Whenever we take a flow in life and analyze the process, we stop the flow. Falling asleep is a great example. If we focus on falling asleep, it becomes very difficult. Instead, if we have that sense of going into something as we are falling asleep, going into the comfort of deeper relaxation, for example, then sleep comes more easily. Surrendering into something stands in contrast to focusing on what we are surrendering.

Through the process of turning our awareness to the heart space, we shift away from the mind and into spatial relationships. We are shifting into the space of the heart's energy. As we explore that space more and more from different angles, we discover all these facets within that space. We come to know the peace that is there, the subtle bliss and light that is there, and the subtle joy and love that radiates within that space. For each of us, it is different at different times. There will be one aspect or another that tends to be more in our awareness, but the heart space allows us this portal into our being. It gives us something to surrender into.

I embrace all of life, knowing all unfolds for the good and for my growth. I embrace all parts of me and reclaim the energy and consciousness I have invested in them and bring them back into Love and into Wholeness. I take Universal Love by the hand and walk side by side and see a higher order to everything. I see the perfection in every flower, in every blade of grass, in every person, and I embrace it all. I love whatever arises, and I sink into the bliss of my full heart. I allow every player in this cosmic play to express themselves and to be fully playing their part. I revel in the knowing that all of this is for me. I see how thousands of events have conspired to push me forth into the greatest growth and an ever greater awareness, Light, and Love. I rest in the peace of the heart and know all is well, all has been for good, and all will be ever unfolding goodness.

Chapter 7

The Bliss: Unconditional Joy

We are standing knee-deep in a river and searching desperately for water. —Kabir Helminski

We often express our desire for others' happiness by encouraging them to enjoy.

"Enjoy the movie."

"Enjoy your family."

"Enjoy your work."

To enjoy is to be *in* joy. Yet, this is not like diving into a pool, it is not that you just "get in" and immediately you are in joy. Enjoying life is central to our health and wellbeing. Still, so many of us are challenged by this and don't find much joy in life. For many, our approach to life is a serious one. We have schedules and demands and responsibilities that need to be met. We have people depending on us and overwhelming societal problems that we face. Life is very serious. Joy is too often the furthest thing from our minds.

I would like to invite you to a different way of being, a different relationship with life, and a different attitude toward living. It has to do with finding joy moment-to-moment. It has to do with finding joy regardless of circumstances. Sounds crazy? Perhaps. As my father used to say, "You don't have to be crazy. But it helps."

Typically our approach to joy is external. We are trying to find something to enjoy. That "thing" is outside of us, and typically in short supply. If you are willing to consider a different way to discover enjoyment in life, then this is what unconditional joy is all about. What if instead of having to wait until your day off to enjoy yourself, you started finding joy in each moment? What if everything you heard was absolutely fascinating to you? Does this sound unrealistic, impossible, or like a fantasy?

Certainly. That is to be expected. Until we have the experience, we often don't think it is possible. To explore this possibility, I will ask you to suspend judgment and consider that for each stage in our growth, the next stage seems impossible. This is where it becomes really interesting though: The human heart is capable of the impossible. If you reflect on it, you'll realize that you've probably already grown in ways that you thought were never possible. Heart centering and heart centered contemplation afford us the possibility of living a life full of presence and joy. That joy is infused into all we do, whether it's work, relationships, study, or even just relaxing. Joy that comes from deep within us radiates into all areas of life. Joy that is present without conditions or external props.

Certainly, stressful times can come, and challenges may be there, but we can meet the challenge and bring energy, liveliness, and joy to the situation. Just like solving a puzzle, we enjoy figuring out how to fit all the pieces together, as we find our way forward. Heart centered living means expanding our awareness of the heart and its facets, living with our awareness more identified and centered in the being that we find at the very core of the heart. From this place, joy becomes the norm.

The importance of joy on our journey cannot be underestimated. The truth of this statement is important to ponder. Joy is essential for health, wealth, and happiness. It is key to relationships too for it is the joy of being with someone that makes relationships rich. It's the joy another takes in our being that creates greater attraction. Joy is infectious; it multiplies itself. And that creates even greater attraction. In a crowd of over 3000 people, Tony Robbins asked the men what the most attractive part of their partner's body was.

The answer, overwhelmingly, was "their smile." And when a man is on-purpose in his life and enjoying his work, there is a confidence that is naturally there that is attractive. Joy wants to be shared.

For so many of us though, we think that love and happiness come from outside of us. Happiness becomes something that we try to "get." Here is where the ego dilemma comes in. The more we need or want something outside of us to make us happy, the more the ego will try to control things so that we can get it. But love that is not spontaneous—that is a response to someone else's ego demand—is unfulfilling because it is just not authentic, it doesn't come freely of its own accord. So if I seek love and happiness outside myself, it doesn't fulfill, and if I do nothing I am unhappy and too often unloved. When we demand something that is only of value if it is freely given, we lose. It is like telling someone to "act natural." If you are acting, you aren't natural. It just doesn't work.

So how do we solve this dilemma? How do we enjoy life without making demands on it? The deeper understanding is that how the ego works can be comprehended easily when we reflect on how the nervous system works. The ego is predominantly associated with those structures and systems that are oriented to our survival. Just as we have a fight-or-flight mechanism to ready our quick response to danger, we also have a system that encourages pleasure and avoids pain. These have connections and associations in the limbic system of the brain where much of emotionality resides. These systems are fairly rooted in survival programming. And they are externally oriented.

So from the ego's perspective, survival is about avoiding pain and finding pleasure. And that is an external game, an outside focus, an environmental orientation. In that world, happiness comes from outside of us—take a drink, take a pill, get a massage, go to a rock concert, get some new music—it is an external orientation. So it becomes logical that the ego seeks outside itself for happiness and takes this "getting" approach. Here is the catch: Love is related to being, not to getting. If any doing is involved, when it comes to love, it is a giving or radiating act.

If life in the ego is not the way to go, then how can we get out of the ego and jump into joy to in-joy life? Through heart centering, of course.

Heart Centering Practice to Discover the Joy of the Heart

In the spaciousness of the heart, in the peace of the True Heart, there is more for us to discover. Tune into the heart centering experience and then sense into the subtle feeling of this space. We can do this most effectively by feeling into the comfort of the peace we find here. Or feeling into the pleasantness of the space. Or by feeling into the liveliness of the expansiveness of this space.

Now for some this aspect of the experience of the subtle heart comes easily. There is a blissfulness or a subtle joy there immediately. The space does not feel empty—it has a fullness to it already. For some this is experienced as a warmth or a glow. For others, though, these experiences seem distant or foreign, as they are more attuned to the spaciousness, expansiveness, or the experience of a void. In that case, there could be a fear of the seeming void. But this is only when the mind assumes that is all there is to the heart. Thankfully, that is just not the case.

As we feel into the comfort, the pleasantness of the peace of the heart, or the liveliness of the spaciousness of the heart, we will need to explore it by going into that experience more deeply. The deeper we go into it and explore it through our subtle perception of the energy, the greater the comfort becomes until we begin to experience a subtle joy. With further exploration, this joy becomes even greater.

When we discover the joy in our own heart and realize it is there available to us, we realize that joy does not have to come from external things. In fact, as we explore further, we come to realize that the joy never came from anything outside of us to begin with. External incentives only served to open our awareness to what was in our heart.

So this is the solution to finding joy even in the most difficult of times. Cultivate the bliss of the heart through this particular process of heart centering. The subtle bliss that will evolve is the foundation for joy. With that foundation firming in our awareness, and with a daily, moment-to-moment practice of heart centering, we come to cultivate joy.

Joy is a key component of Universal Love. It provides feedback on whether we're on track with our life purpose and our life lessons. In that way, it becomes an amazing barometer for us. The basis for celebrating all of life finds its roots in joy. One of the things that few realize is that when we're radiating joy, it is highly attractive. It attracts all sorts of goodness. It attracts all sorts of favor. It attracts all sorts of abundance. It can attract to us others who want to share in that flow of joyous celebration with us. In a sense, as we move forward in our inner growth, joy is no longer a luxury; it is essential feedback on our progress.

As we cultivate the heart and expand our awareness, we find within every moment blissfulness, or awe, or innocent curiosity that makes that moment joyful. We find we can be in bliss, we can be in joy even in the midst of a whole wide range of emotions, and we discover the beauty within emotional flow itself. We can find beauty and joy in being able to care for and cherish others, to cherish our ability to love and to be involved with and care about life.

Our joy expresses greater, unconditional joy into the world. Too often we have reserved joy for those moments of accomplishment or fulfillment of a desire. As we begin to use our full potential, joy is not just a reward. Instead, we discover within every element of our experience that bliss is available at every point in space and time. In other words, the flow of the energy of Universal Love exists everywhere. Cultivating our intuition, our ability to sense this energy subtly, makes all the difference. As we do so, we come to understand that bliss is always available and Universal Love is always present—unconditionally.

Evolved souls such as Eckhart Tolle know this. When answering a question about whether he still has thoughts, he said, yes, but he can also just sit and look out a window for 25 minutes in silence. Why can he do this? Because every moment is fascinating. There's no need to be constantly thinking and analyzing and talking to oneself. When we expand our awareness of the bliss and Universal Love that is ever-present, life becomes totally fascinating. Every object, everything that we perceive with our senses becomes enchanting. Just stopping thinking misses the point; the point is that as we become aware, joy is increasingly available. Then every aspect of life becomes worthy of celebration.

Now, many times in my life, I've felt frustrated that the world is progressing so slowly, and that's a good thing. Let me explain why. It caused great suffering that pushed me forward and caused me to grow. And it was when I had grown enough and become aware enough of that Light and Love within, that I could sit with that desire for a better world. I could then recognize that it was blissful to have that desire, that it was a wonderful thing to have. It has been a wonderful tool, a wonderful motivator for me. And at this point, I could enjoy just the desire, rather than insisting that the Universe fulfill it immediately and in the exact way that I wanted it to be fulfilled. In this way, I learned that every aspect of life—whether it's a challenge, whether it is an emotion, whether it's a difficult relationship—can take on a different quality that can be cherished when we become aware of the bliss of being and the presence of Universal Love. When we begin to shift identification from, "I am this person and this thing is happening to me," to "I am Light and Love fascinated by what is happening and excited to be expressing my unique Divinity in this moment," everything can bring joy.

This is what makes the mystics talk about the inexplicable pull, the seductiveness of the Divine. Too often this gets misinterpreted as a pull towards isolation or becoming a recluse. That's because it's not in the world; it is within you. Especially, it's not in the fulfillment of desire that we find happiness ultimately. We tend to learn that by seeking it in all the wrong places. As Kabir Helminski writes, "We are knee deep in a river, crying out for water." What we're seeking is within us. What we're seeking is within us with every desire.

All of these things in life are permission slips for us to relax into the bliss of being. They each allow an opening to unconditional joy, once we realize the joy is not in getting what we want. That doesn't mean we can't enjoy worldly things. Once the anxiety about not getting what we want fades, we are actually free to enjoy getting what we want even more. The key, though, is to discover that our joy is not conditional, it doesn't depend on externals. We discover the bliss of being within our own heart, and all tends to shift.

When that happens, it can be very seductive to think of just going away and sitting in the bliss. Few of us are really here to do that; most of us are here to express our Light and joy into the world. We are to be blossoming in our unique and creative way and bringing that into the world, so that it can be a world of beauty. Rediscovering the bliss of being that we often see in children, we create unconditional joy. In children, it is present in an unconscious way. We are coming to a conscious expression of joy. This is what we are uncovering. It doesn't come from philosophy. It doesn't come from a teacher or a master or guru. It is an uncovering that comes through grace, through your own development of awareness.

All of the worldly things that create joy are wonderful. Awakening the heart doesn't mean that it's time to let those go. It doesn't mean that we discount them as just being superficial. When we expand our awareness, the intensity of desire and the bliss of fulfilling it becomes greater. It has power behind it, and it's part of what we're here for. It's the expansion of creation, the expansion of love. When we love life, love what we're eating, love what we are doing, and love each other—all of that creates an expansion of love. This fulfills the purpose of creation. That greater expansion of love is the reason creation created individual beings—so that Universal Love could create even more love.

Ultimately, how all of this takes place for any given individual is a fascinating story, each of us having our own story and our own path, aimed at coming to be a fuller expression of the Universal Light and Love we carry within. In that sense, joy is part of our most fundamental nature. That's why joy is that feedback that we're in alignment with our purpose. When we are in joy, we are coming closer and closer to our true self, and that is worth celebrating.

The old foundation for joy was obtaining power so we could get more of what we wanted. Power in the form of more money, more authority, and more worldly influence. The new foundation for joy is cultivating the heart through expansion of awareness and intuitive perception. This allows us to base joy on being rather than on accomplishments. When we look at Dean Ornish's research on treating cardiovascular disease without drugs, he found that many of the people in his first studies were extremely successful and powerful. They were successful, often married, and yet felt quite lonely and disconnected from themselves. So as part of his program, in addition to exercising and following a plant-based diet, every person had couples counseling. Accomplishments don't make us happy, the joy they bring is conditional. Happiness has more to do with the flow of love. Unhappiness creates stress and strain; Ornish insisted on couples counseling to create real joy and happiness in the lives of these otherwise successful individuals. With this program Ornish succeeded where the medical profession thought he would fail. He proved the power of love could create health and aid in reversing heart disease.

The external approach applies equally to addictions. Addictions are very seductive, the momentary pleasure that we keep coming back to is not true joy but it creates a strong association in the mind. Addictions will never bring lasting fulfillment because they don't connect to Universal Love and to the bliss of being. They distract us from pain, and in the process, they distract us even more from unconditional joy.

What we are seeking through desire motivates us to grow and evolve until we come to know the Universal Love and Light within, that we actually are. Once knowing that on an experiential level, unconditional joy begins to shine through every experience and every step we take. Through cultivating the heart, we begin to live the fullness of life and can truly ENJOY!

Chapter 8

The One Heart: Complete Forgiveness and Compassion

In 2015, a young American man by the name of Salahuddin Jitmoud was making his final delivery of pizza for the night. Three men lured him into their apartment complex and then robbed and stabbed him to death. At the sentencing for his son's murderer, Jitmoud's father, a school principal and devout Muslim, asked the judge if he could address his son's murderer directly. The judge granted this request and had him sworn in, and he addressed the man in front of the entire court with the murderer's family looking on. He said, "I feel so—so sad for you that you have to be in this situation. I wish I could help you, as I helped my son to be a good citizen. If Salahuddin were to be here, if he were alive, he would forgive you. That is the way he was. That is the way he is." Then he went on to say, "I'm not angry at you at all. I want you to know that. I forgive you on behalf of Salahuddin and his mother." The murderer then was given the chance to address the court. He began to cry and amidst his appreciation for this man's courage, heart, and ability to forgive, they ended up *hugging each other. (This is one of the most moving things you will ever see: YouTube Video: https://youtu.be/8wifYHbVl9c?feature=shared — Scan code is below)*

The power of forgiveness comes in freeing oneself from the pain of blame and judgment. It comes in turning things over to a Higher Power. It comes in choosing peace over anger, love over hate, and freedom over being forever bound to those we judge.

It is difficult to understand the power of forgiveness without the direct experience of full forgiveness. The context for understanding full forgiveness and the power it gives is very much grounded in the human nervous system and how the brain works. For this reason, we will briefly review earlier information, but this time in the specific context of forgiveness. We are not the brain; the brain is a tool through which we interact with physical reality. We have a way of processing that hides the tool from our awareness. Thus, we don't know that we have developed our ability to interpret reality, we don't see that "reality" is very much a conditioned interpretation for most of us. It is something that is perceived by using only a part of the brain—the left brain.

From a neurological perspective, we essentially have two different modes for understanding and experiencing reality. That is because the brain is divided into two hemispheres and each one is responsible for very different functions. Why is this important? Because how we perceive reality has a lot to do with what we find unacceptable, which has a lot to do with how much we suffer. All of that is essential to understanding forgiveness. To give an even broader context, the enlightened sages of the past were often referred to as "the knowers of reality." They were able to perceive the wholeness of life and all of creation—they had full perception of reality. They were able to perceive all interconnections and had the broadest possible vision of life. They knew completely who and what we are. They did this through their inner growth and development. This was reflected in a very integrated style of perception—one that combined both right and left hemispheres.

Language and all of the concepts of language, as well as all of our concepts of linear time, reside in the left brain. We have a concept of the past, present, and future. We can use our concept of the past to inform the present and to try to predict the future. This is often where unforgiveness comes in. Something painful has happened in the past, and we want to make sure that it doesn't happen again in the future. That part of the function of the left brain is connected with survival and our egoic sense of self. When something painful happens, we try to protect ourselves from it in the future. So we learn to judge people and situations as "good" or "bad." This serves to help us distinguish who and what to be around. It also further bolsters our self-concept as being "good" and staying safe and secure.

From that, we create a set of concepts about ourselves, concepts of right and wrong, which are very much language-bound and very much a left-brain perception of reality. The problem comes in that we live in the past, which is a concept—each evaluation and judgment then binds us to the past experience of pain and recreates it subconsciously. We live in fear of the past repeating.

There is a caveat here; all of this is not to say that our survival instinct and protecting ourselves is to be thrown out. The left-brain functions are important in ensuring we maintain our ability to function in the world. However, we are learning to integrate and live from the whole brain, while allowing the right brain to drive, particularly when it comes to forgiveness. Integrated living will bring us to a point of discernment and a healthy place of knowing right from wrong without the unhelpful judgments, grudges, and assumptions that keep us stuck, seeing reality through narrow lenses.

Left to their own devices, all of these functions of the left brain that we have discussed, make it very hard to talk ourselves into forgiveness. It simply goes against the way we have been trained to see the world. It also goes against the way the ego and the left brain function. Our best hope for forgiveness comes from the right brain. The right brain is silent. No language or concepts exist there. The right brain is where we experience the timelessness of the true Reality. This is where we find those functions related to inner peace and inner freedom, without which we cannot come to forgiveness. It's where those functions related to love are located. And it explains why a real depth of love can take us to a timeless place, much like it did for Salahuddin's father.

The fastest path to forgiveness is to access inner peace and freedom through the tool of the right brain. It is to come to the bliss of being through our presence in this moment. Presence brings in the liveliness of Spirit and Divinity, and from that reality, forgiveness takes on a whole different context. From that reality, we step out of suffering and can look carefully at the assumptions and the prison built through nonforgiveness.

Remember how Jill Bolte Taylor, the neuroscientist who had a stroke that affected her left-brain functioning, said that in an instant her stroke wiped out decades of emotional baggage? She experienced the timelessness of the right brain, which meant she could forgive. The right brain is responsible for that perception of ourselves and life beyond emotional baggage. In meditation, the left brain becomes quieter and the right brain comes to the forefront. When we heart center, we orient to the heart space and that accesses more of the right brain and the cerebellar spatial orientation. This also allows the left brain to settle, resulting in perception that is more realistic, holistic, and accurate. We perceive who we truly are beyond language, concept, and the confines of our past.

When we begin to loosen our identification with our concepts and thoughts, we begin to know ourselves as spaciousness, heartfulness, and blissfulness. This self-knowledge gives us an important foundation for any spiritual practice, especially the practice of forgiveness.

Without that experience and foundation, we truly are in a battle with ourselves. The battle is tough as the nature of the left brain is to be oriented towards our survival, so we resist letting go of it. The left brain is also intimately connected to our emotional body. Our perception is therefore organized around getting our needs met, creating safety, and ensuring our survival.

Given that context, when something happens that we judge as threatening or "wrong," it is subconsciously tied to fear—it kicks in the survival thinking. We try to sort out what is safe and what is not. Who can I trust? Who is reliable? This processing, by its very nature, takes us into judgment. That fixes and strengthens our past perception. Forgiveness becomes difficult because from the left-brain perspective, it means going against our basic needs—our survival instincts and the subconscious programming that we have created. We can chase ourselves in circles trying to forgive and then beat up on ourselves repeatedly for not doing so—all to no avail. It rarely changes anything.

Rather than fighting with ourselves, and then having to forgive ourselves for not being able to forgive, the solution is to step outside of the ego and explore the heart space. Within the spaciousness and unboundedness of the heart space, we enter our being and discover the right-brain dominant presence that Jill Bolte Taylor described and that Salahuddin's father displayed. From here, it is easy to let go and forgive because we are already in a surrendered place. We are out of the subconscious associations and resting in the power of presence.

In this way, we don't need to make more rules for the ego to try to be non-egoic. Instead, we make the right-brain experience the foundation for intuitive insight. We make it a foundation for forgiveness and letting go to be natural and easy. Doing so, we begin to live more wholeness, blissfulness, and peacefulness. Any grudge we hold starts to feel uncomfortable, and we just prefer to let it go. This leads us to the infinite expansiveness of our being where we realize that each of us is a wave in the ocean of consciousness. We recognize that, like an ocean that can have many, many different waves, regardless of how many waves there are, there is just one ocean. Each of us is a wave in the ocean of consciousness. With that realization, it becomes very easy to forgive, because we are just forgiving ourselves.

Developing the habit of getting out of the left brain through exploring the heart space allows us to become aware of the expansiveness and peacefulness within. It allows us to be present to what is real. Then it becomes easy to let go and to forgive. Don't worry, you will not lose your left-brain capacity for survival, you will in fact see more of reality, not less. But making forgiveness easy is important. Why? Because when we can't forgive, we are bound to someone else and we lose our power. Someone else's past actions remain in control of our internal state. When we forgive, we reclaim our power and set ourselves free. As a byproduct of the process, the other person is set free from our influence and judgment.

When we can't forgive, it dominates our reality and we miss out on much of life. We don't see the full reality. We don't live in the present moment, and the bliss of being is overshadowed. That causes us to seek bliss and joy, once again through the fulfillment of desires, an approach we have explored in previous chapters, which rarely works. We become less and less free and at peace. Liberation comes when we are able to live more from the right-brain perception, beyond concept and old programming—free of the past. This doesn't mean that we do not honor the past, it does not mean that we forget the past or discount it as unreal. All experiences encompass our reality in a timeless sense. When we live from left-brain programming, however, we are guaranteed to repeat the past and get lost in it, unable to find presence. We think the same thoughts we had previously and repeat the same behaviors and emotions over and over again. In a way, this is dishonoring to the past as we do not allow these experiences that are in our awareness to serve our growth and evolution. Instead of being present to them and drawing wisdom from them, we get stuck in the flat concept of the past. If we become present to them, insights for our inner development will arise in our present experience.

An unwillingness or inability to let go of judgment and forgive keeps us from being free to put our attention where we wish. It hinders our ability to determine our inner experience. Whatever behavior occurred or words were said, they live on in us and determine our mental-emotional state. Through the process of identification, our mental-emotional experience begins to determine who we are. We give over all of our power to that person or situation that we judge.

Someone may have borrowed money from us and never returned it. If we judge by thinking, "that person is irresponsible," or "that person is dishonest," then we create a reaction in our nervous system that is unpleasant. We allow our perception of that person's behavior to determine our internal state. This is the fascinating thing about the way the body is organized. Whenever we judge, whenever we get irritated or angry with someone else, the body—our body—takes the first blow. We create stress biochemicals that affect our organs. It is our body that suffers and our experience that becomes unpleasant. So we suffer.

When we hang on to judgments and refuse to forgive, it's not the other person who continues to suffer. Too much of the left-brain programming that involves judgment is based on a belief in punishment. We don't realize there are cultures where there is no concept of punishment. Too often we hold the belief, consciously or subconsciously, that when somebody does something wrong, they deserve to be punished; if we don't punish them, somebody should or "they will never learn." We hold this belief in spite of every study in the field of psychology pointing to the fact that punishment doesn't work. Punishment doesn't modify behavior; it basically makes people afraid of the person who doles out the punishment. It is incredibly ineffective at changing behavior.

The mind says, "Judging is a good thing—it will protect me." This is based on the belief that next time I'll be able to make a distinction between this person and that person. I'll know to avoid that person because I can judge whether they're responsible or irresponsible. The illusion that judgment serves and protects me is just that—illusion. Judgment binds us to the past, attracting like situations as we insist on kindling that energy. It binds us to others. It puts us into a cage. Walls of protection, layer upon layer, only make us prisoners of our own mind. Judgment puts us in jail. It keeps us from being free to respond in any way we choose. It keeps us from creating happiness in any situation by choice.

A Culture Without Punishment

At an integrative medical conference focused on healing the planet, one of the most well-received speakers was an elder of the Inuit tribe. He talked about his introduction to nature from his grandfather. He talked about how his parents reared him. They never spoke a negative word to him. They never discouraged him. They never punished him. Punishment was just not the way of his people or his culture.

He told an amazing story about when he was very young and when he walked by the hardware store in his town, which was like a general store. He saw this toy truck in the window, and he very much wanted this truck. One day he went into the store and he bought the truck. On the way out of the store while walking down the street, he bumped into his aunt. His aunt approached him and said, "Oh, I see you have bought something. What did you get?" He said he really wanted this truck so he bought it.

"Oh, where did you get the money for the truck?"

"I took it from my father's dresser."

She looked at him and said, "Oh, well what do you think you should do about that?"

He fell silent for a moment. Then he said, "I think I probably should take the truck back and get a refund and give dad his money back."

She said, "Good boy," and she went on walking down the street.

He described how children in his culture were seen as an embodiment of the Divine Spirit. As such, it was considered an insult to the Divine Spirit to punish or criticize children. The entire culture was organized around this principle. So when he was growing up, if he was engaging in unhelpful behavior, they would just turn away from him. They wouldn't say anything negative. They would just turn their backs to him. That is how he was raised. No punishment. No criticism. No concept of a person having the capacity to be something negative.

In some cultures, people are seen as a process, not a thing. If you were to say, "He is dumb or she is dumb," it is incomprehensible to them. They don't think of a person as a "thing" that has qualities. They see people as work in progress and as a process. This is very hard for many of us to grasp. In these people, the subconscious, left-brain programming is devoid of judgment. Instead, there is a capacity for discernment. They can see the differences between behaviors, but there's no judgment and as a result, there's no need to forgive.

The task in evolving humanity at this time is learning to think with the heart and love with the mind. It is about reprogramming the mind, such that fear, judgment, and lack of forgiveness are no longer part of our subconscious mind. Then love, peace, and truth will dominate our thinking. Thinking with the heart means we think intuitively and perceive directly without analysis. We cognize or download truth. We allow ourselves to be centered and in the freedom that exists, as we use the heart space as a portal into the essence of our being. In that, we can come to complete freedom and liberation from all that pains us and creates suffering.

For some of us, self-forgiveness is the hardest. Too often we treat ourselves as an object. Then we describe that object in negative terms, all the while not realizing that this way of thinking is not natural. It is something absorbed from our culture and upbringing. We have internalized it from others with good intentions. We have convinced ourselves that it is the way to be a better person.

We thought emulating those who judge would help us to be better. Thus, we set out to whip ourselves into shape. We undertake a project of improving ourselves by berating ourselves. We punish ourselves by feeling guilty and describing ourselves in negative terms—all based on the illusion that this is how we change. It starts with an assumption that we have to be forced to change. The reality is that we are a continually unfolding and flowing process. That process is best influenced by the heart that connects to our higher wisdom. It's the heart that is the gateway to the Higher Self and to higher consciousness.

The importance of heart centering and exploring the heart space cannot be overemphasized. These practices are a doorway into our being and coming to know that True Self. They offer the direct knowing that we are one with everyone. Judgment assumes that we are isolated. It assumes that others are not us and that they are different and bad. When we directly experience an expansive sense of oneness with others, judgment falls away. Fearing others is not needed. Fearing their behavior is not needed. Making them out to be bad is a foreign concept. This is the power of exploring the heart space—we discover the Universal Heart that we all share.

In that process, we come to know the light, the expansiveness, and the freedom of our being. We also become aware of the amazing process of growth that is unfolding, that we call a person. From that vantage point, we can experience our true power and our true freedom. The point of power is to be free to create what we want. The point of power is to be able to determine the quality of our existence.

When we center in the heart space and reclaim our power from those fears that have been programmed into the mind as judgments, we heal the past and begin living with more presence. The fears of the past are healed because the antidote to fear is love. We are using the connection to Divine Love—the heart space—to heal fear. It is not the mind that heals, it is not analysis that heals; it is the deep self-compassion that creates healing beyond our intellectual comprehension. It is the fullness of compassion and the sense of oneness that makes forgiveness complete. Exploring the heart space also allows us to discover the bliss of being. We come to discover the true being that we are, the Self that we are, and that in and of itself is healing. This all creates growth, more light—enlightening us, bit by bit.

We can see how inner growth, healing, and enlightenment are all intertwined. They are all one and the same thing. Engaging in that growth fosters a strengthening of our sense of self as we reclaim the energy we have invested in judgments and in the past. We experience greater freedom, liveliness, and happiness. We experience joy for absolutely no reason. We become free. We have the power to determine our inner experience and we can create a life that is beyond our wildest imagination. So becoming free is a process of reclaiming our power, stepping out of the mind, and shifting identification.

When we think, "I've been wrong," or "I was hurt," the mind has a concept of "I" that is assumed. Everything is in relation to this "I." We become absorbed in these events, and we assume they happened to this "I." We identify completely with the "I" in the story of what happened. That identification with the ego creates a concept of an isolated self that needs to protect itself. It stands in stark contrast to our direct right-brain experience of the spaciousness within us. It is totally different from our sense of ourselves that comes when we use the heart space as a portal into our being. It pales in comparison to the direct experience of ourselves that we have in meditation. When we come to that point in meditation where things become very quiet, we directly experience who we are. We let go of that sense of self built on a concept of a me to which something happened. If we continue to pour our attention and consciousness into that egoic sense of self, we strengthen our identification with those concepts. That "me" seems more and more real. Then we are bound by unforgiveness.

When we come out of thinking and into the heart, we experience a bigger sense of self. We go beyond a limited sense of "me." We become present, and in that presence, nothing can touch or impact our real Self.

How Compassion Flows from the One Heart

As we come to know ourselves as Light and Love, we become aware of the Divine flow within the ocean of consciousness. We discover a fabric within consciousness itself. Interwoven is bliss. When bliss flows, love grows. Joy and happiness are the result. With the full compassion born of this shift in identification comes complete forgiveness.

Being in a constant state of forgiveness, of "giving over," or "fore-giving" becomes natural. We constantly give over whatever arises. We constantly send loving energy to whatever arises. If it is a thought, we send loving energy to it. If it is an emotion, we become fully present to it and send loving energy to it. If it is some hurt, we send loving energy to it and it heals. In that sense, we love everything that arises.

As we practice this continual forgiveness, we become so identified with the love that we are, that nothing else can grab our mind and pull us back into the illusion of a static "me." We have then created the foundation for living an enlightened life.

Full forgiveness removes all blocks to compassion. Full forgiveness allows the natural flow of compassion to come forth. It opens us to our true nature. It makes compassion spontaneous, full, and complete.

The standard thinking is that compassion is something that we "do." While whatever brings us to greater compassion is valuable, "doing compassion" takes us back into the ego and obscures the natural expression of our deeper nature. Compassion is an expression of who we actually are. Forcing compassion, in exactly the same way as forcing forgiveness, from the mind gets us tied in knots. When compassion becomes a more mental "doing," it becomes very stale—it doesn't feel authentic. When it arises naturally out of the heart, from that state of being, we spontaneously express our nature, which is loving and compassionate. All of this doesn't come from the mind. To allow it to unfold permanently requires retraining and reprogramming of the mind; however, rather than starting with training the mind, we recognize that the mind will get trained as we experience life differently. Experience shifts our perceptions, and that shifts our thinking. It also shifts our way of reacting to our emotional responses.

Through the oneness in the heart space, we come to a feeling of the Universal Heart. In oneness, we have a sense that while there are many minds, there is one heart that is shared by humanity. Without the experience, this is difficult to understand; with the experience of the sense of oneness, it becomes comprehensible. From this, arises a knowing that it would be unthinkable to do anything that would harm someone else. It is simply not in our nature, harming ourselves is not aligned with our nature. We begin to recognize that others are different expressions of the one heart—they are an expression of us.

Complete compassion and understanding are the true expressions of the one heart. The power of this one heart is exemplified by Dannion Brinkley, author of the book Saved by the Light.

Brinkley was struck by lightning and had severe internal burns and damage to his heart. He actually died as a result; he was clinically dead for about 25 minutes, during which he went through a life review. He describes in exquisite detail how during that life review, consciousness is expanded, so that he not only experienced what he did all over again, but also simultaneously what those around him were feeling and experiencing.

This was particularly difficult to watch because he was a bully in high school. He felt all of the anger he had from how he had been treated as a child, which propelled him to beat up on someone else. He simultaneously experienced the humiliation of being beaten up and the pain, both emotional and physical, associated with his actions.

Brinkley went into the military and became a sniper in Vietnam. In his life review, as he shot a Vietnamese lieutenant colonel, he simultaneously felt himself squeezing the trigger and the pain of the lieutenant colonel's realization that he had been shot and would never see his loved ones again. Then he experienced the horror and pain the family experienced when learning that their loved one had just been shot to death. All of this occurred simultaneously.

This is the sense of the one heart and the reality that we are all one in terms of consciousness. When we experience this one heart, it changes everything. We lift the filters of the mind and begin to perceive the beauty of people and the reality that they are us. Exploring the heart space gives us a window into this greater reality. The heart is the portal into our greater being. The heart can reflect this greater unity, as it is its nature to unify and bring things into harmony.

The heart reflects the truth of our being and the truth of Divinity, which is that it is the force of evolution. It is our nature to grow, develop, and seek greater and greater happiness, love, and expressions of the Divinity that we are. While we often think of compassion benefiting others, the deepest compassion cannot help but benefit us. Why is that? When we see tragedy, we will suffer, unless we can hold the world with compassion in our heart. We need to be that Divine Mother or Father that holds the entire world, just like a mother or father holds a child when they fall and scrape their knee. We might be unable to do anything about what has happened, but we have the ability to hold that child and comfort them with our love.

When we expand this ability to be anchored in the heart and in the sense of oneness, we allow compassion to flow. Then the suffering of the world and all of the tragedies don't have to bring us down. Instead, they allow us to experience the truth of our being and our ability to bring forth the Light and Love into the world. This doesn't mean we don't care. It doesn't mean that we justify what is. What it does mean is that we are able to be in the flow of Universal Love and be a positive healing influence.

Compassion doesn't just benefit those around us; it heals us. It makes us whole again. It allows us to cultivate the heart and live in greater awareness and flow. It brings us to a greater wholeness and a broader reality. It helps us reclaim all the energy that we've invested in judgment, criticism, and resistance. That allows us to hold even more within our heart. Compassion brings us to an experience of oneness that reverberates on each level of our being—physical, energetic, emotional, mental, causal, and spiritual, creating a channel for pure light, pure consciousness, and pure love.

Conclusion

Your Relationship with Universal Love

"Love is the strongest medicine. It can heal the most wounded heart and soothe the most restless soul." —Rumi

To Everything Radiate Love

This is the essence of any path of love: To everything radiate love. This path of joy and radiance is simple once you have the awareness of the subtle energy of love. It is simple once you recognize this energy as an aspect of your being. It becomes simple because it creates joy. It creates happiness. It heals and alleviates suffering. Most importantly, it creates a shift in identification. As we radiate love, we realize that we are love.

To everything radiate love—especially to fear. Love in this sense is the antidote to fear. Fear speaks to a false reality of disconnection. It relies on us having an isolated sense of self that is threatened by the thing we fear. "Our needs won't get met, our security will be destroyed, we will lose external approval and acceptance" —all of these are based on the concept that we are separate, isolated, disconnected, and mortal beings. Love says the opposite.

When we radiate love to fear, it begins to soften. Love harmonizes and connects by its very nature. When we radiate love to fear, we begin to connect to the Universal, we begin to identify more with the love and the being that is radiating it, rather than the fear and concept of a personality that is threatened. Love heals fear. It connects us to a Higher Order and allows us to put fear in its place; we can see it as a function of the body trying to preserve itself. That has a time and a place. We can love and honor that, but not allow it to run the show. From the standpoint of radiating love, we can choose how we want to relate to the fear—we can bring Light to it in the form of wisdom, and from there, we are free to heed its warnings or recognize the illusion that it is gripped by. Often in that wisdom, the illusion is dropped and the fear subsides.

Radiating love to fear has nothing to do with "liking" or "approving" of fear. As is the case with true love, no evaluation is involved. We radiate love because it is our nature. We radiate love because it uplifts us and brings happiness. The alternative—resisting fear—ends in either a great struggle where the resistance intensifies the fear, or in repression where the fear persists in the background undermining our energy and our health. Radiating love to fear is like wrapping it in a warm blanket. It is like a mother who scoops the child who has skinned his or her knee up into her arms. The love lets the child know it is all going to be okay. As we radiate the essence of peace and bliss to our fear, it has this healing and soothing effect. We are fully present to it. We don't repress or suppress it. The energy of love heals it. It reconnects this fragmented part of us with the greater being that we are.

When we truly radiate love with intensity, we become absorbed in it, and our identification shifts. We become it. Then fear floats away. Love heals fear. It opens us to insight. It opens us to a more accurate perception of reality. It brings us to peace. It takes us out of suffering. What greater skill and practice is there?

What About the Ego?

"What an awful thing to have an ego." So goes many teachings. The quest becomes the effort to destroy the ego. This is a negative approach to growth, full of ascetic tendencies and withdrawal from life. This is almost always impossible, as ego is just a manifestation of consciousness. This is why Evelyn Underhill in her works on mysticism talks about the rebuilding of the personality, not the complete destroying or obliterating of it. To be able to relate to others and to function in the world, a personality is needed. When we love the ego, or our mental-emotional sense of ourselves, the fear that is at its core leaves and the personality remains.

This personality can now be aligned with Light and Love. More accurately, the personality can now be a tool of the Light and Love. The ego can take the back seat and allow a spirit-filled soul to run the show.

The Most Important Relationship

Our relationship with ourselves is important. It is often our primary focus as we begin to become more aware. However, as we discover the Universal Love within us and come to know fully who we are, it becomes less and less important. We work through the ego patterns and blocks that take us out of awareness, and we stop punishing ourselves or evaluating ourselves as we experience our true worth as an expression of the Bliss, Light, and Love within—as we discover our True Divine nature. This discovery is the first and foundational step in cultivating a greater relationship with life and with the source of life. This discovery takes place as we cultivate the heart and the intuitive perception of the energy of love within.

Once we become aware of our greater self, many of the problems and challenges in life get resolved or simply fall away. We then have a foundation for knowing life at a deeper level. We become aware of the Bliss, Light, and Love that is outside of us. This starts in a subtle way. We start to see colors as more vibrant. We discover that vibrancy is the Light of Universal Love shining through, making our perception incredibly clear and refined. We start to feel a greater presence as well. Increasingly, we come to be aware that the Bliss, Light, and Love within us exist outside of us. In fact, we begin to feel it radiating to us in an ever-present, glorious, and loving way.

When this realization comes, it is stunning, life-changing, moving. It can move us to tears. This awakening of the heart allows us to become aware of a connectedness to the entire Universe, as Bliss, Light, and Love are everywhere, shining forth and radiating to us. Once we realize the source of that radiance, we can begin the most intimate and loving relationship to the Source of All That Is.

This begins the final step in developing the most important relationship you will ever have. The fullness of heart that results is ecstatic, the gratitude overwhelming. We come repeatedly to a sense of Unity with this love, all of life is transformed. All suffering falls away. The sense of coming home is total and complete. The love is glorious beyond words. As Rumi said, "Be drunk in love, since love is everything that exists."

In the beginning of this book, I spoke about a bold transformation and a call for a new approach to life, success, and spirituality. An approach not based on belief or ritual, but on the experience of the most powerful force in the Universe. We have explored the experience of this most powerful force, Universal

Love, which is accessible through our human heart space. With the practice of heart centering, the repeated turning of awareness to the heart space, we develop the basis for spiritual practice in our own experience. In this manner, the spiritual practices become a spontaneous expression of our internal experience.

It is my hope that you are inspired to awaken your heart and further explore and deepen your experience of the peace, bliss, and oneness of Universal Love within and outside of you.

Contemplations

The Facets of the Heart

The Facets of the Heart, the qualities and experiences of the One Spiritual Heart, that will spontaneously unfold and overflow into your lived experience as you continue on this path are important to recognize. I invite you to shift your awareness to the heart space and contemplate each of these facets with the verses in the following pages and to feel into the qualities and experiences that naturally arise in your awareness. Under each contemplation title is the quality you will find in the heart space followed by what develops as we contemplate that quality and what it implies for our life. All the facets are interwoven; develop any one of them, and the others will come along. Follow your own experience and if you feel called to, then use the affirmation at the end of each contemplation. (You can also close your eyes and hear these contemplations read by me using the scan code below.)

The Facets of the Heart

Radical acceptance, unshakeable faith, loving presence, grace, inner guidance, unconditional joy, true appreciation, gratitude, generosity, radiance healing, total forgiveness, and full compassion.

Never underestimate the treasure that you hold within you—the power of awareness and the power of the heart. Every wave in the ocean affects the entire ocean, sending a ripple effect throughout eternity. We are growing not just for ourselves; we are growing and uplifting all of humanity. One of my favorite quotes from Shirley MacLaine's Out on a Limb is this: "The progress that any individual makes in any given lifetime uplifts all of humanity for all of time." That is how important what you are doing with practicing heart centering and coming to know the Universal Spiritual Heart is—that is *how important you are to the world.* You have the right keys. Now let your life be a fascinating discovery.

Radical Acceptance

Peace ~ Acceptance ~ Radical Acceptance

In the clear perception of peace within my own heart space, I revel in the freedom peace brings.

I experience complete freedom from fear. All pressure goes away.

I require nothing of the world for I am anchored in the silence of my being.

Everything settles and I ground into the peace like it is all that I know, all that has ever been, and all that will ever be.

All resistance fades and the mind becomes distant and less active.

I am solid, safe, and knowing only the peace—a peace that does "passeth all understanding."

I have no impulse to resist anything. I am at peace with whatever arises.

I accept everything and resist nothing.

I have no impulse to resist even that which I do not like or don't want because I am this peace and this peace is me. Everything else is superficial.

From here, I open up and allow the mind to entertain the possibility that everything that comes to me in life is FOR ME.

Within this peace and settledness, I come to a knowingness—I can embrace whatever arises.

I am at peace with whatever arises. I can love whatever arises.

This knowingness is not a mental belief, it is a truth that resonates deeply with the peace within.

Affirmation

I am peace and from my essence I embrace everything.

Unshakeable Faith

Peace ~ Centeredness ~ Surrender ~ Unshakeable Faith

As I feel into the depth of the peace within, I discover a solid groundedness.

As I keep coming back to this, I am truly centered.

The more I reside here, the more comfortable it is. I reside in the peace and centeredness.

In this awareness of my being, through the portal of the heart space, I am unshakeable.

I find a home within myself—a coming home to something greater.

Whatever comes, I can let go and return here. I can surrender anything, simply by coming home again.

Whatever it is, whatever thought or judgment, like or dislike, desire or preference,

I can surrender it by letting go into the depth of the peace within my own heart and being.

As I encounter situation after situation with this sense of ultimate surrender and peace,

I know all will be well. I come to the foundation of faith itself.

In the unshakeable centeredness and inner peace,

I have absolute faith that all is unfolding exactly how it is meant to be.

Affirmation

With the unshakeable peace of my being, I have faith that all is unfolding perfectly.

Loving Presence

Peace ~ Innocence and Liveliness ~ Presence ~ Loving Presence

Shifting my awareness to the peace within, during my day, I notice a clarity and an innocence.

Each moment seems vibrant and lively. My thoughts dominate less.

They slow, and I am fully aware and deeply fascinated by everything I see and everyone I interact with.

This liveliness and vibrancy is palpable and it brings with it a total presence.

This is more than just "being in the moment."

The liveliness of Universal Love shines through each moment,

and with it "being present" is transformed into loving presence.

I am in the flow of something greater, fully awake and deeply aware.

This flow of loving presence transforms every moment, every thought, and every perception.

It can only be described as awesome.

Affirmation

With peace in my heart, I am in the flow of loving presence.

Grace

Peace ~ Permanence ~ Invincibility ~ Grace

Every time I shift my awareness to the heart space, I rediscover the peace within.

As I contemplate this, it becomes clear—it is always there.

No matter what I do to distract myself from it, no matter what I do to cover it over,

I can always find my way back to it.

When I do, the "I" disappears and the permanence of the peace is all that is present.

It is untouchable—permanent, and cannot be destroyed. It is always there.

This invincible peace dispels every insecurity, every uncertainty, and it opens me to the flow of grace.

With the ego's "I" taking a break and residing on the sideline, uncertainty, fear, and doubt disappear,

and the permanence of the peace within is apparent.

I open to the flow of life and Universal Love and grace follow.

Affirmation

I open to invincible peace and to the flow of Universal Love and grace.

Inner Guidance

Peace ~ Alignment ~ Harmony ~ Inner Guidance

Within the quiet and peace of my innermost heart, I notice a clarifying of intuition.

I notice this settling and grounding effect whenever intuitive inspiration comes.

It is how I know the difference between a random thought and true intuition—a settledness and sense of peace is present with it,

as if to say, "Yes, this is in harmony."

A sense of alignment and harmony is present within the inner peace.

As I rest in the peace, the quiet opens me to clearer intuitive knowing.

With any decision, I can bring it into the peace

and feel an increase in settledness when it is aligned, or a flatness or roughness when it is not.

As I shift my awareness to the heart space, and through that, to the peace within,

I then come to inner guidance, having the sense of harmony clearly in my awareness.

I know what takes me out of it. I know what emotions are not aligned with it,

and I see through the beliefs that are no longer aligned with the truth of my being.

Affirmation

Inner guidance flows in the peace of my innermost heart.

Unconditional Joy

Bliss ~ Joy ~ Unconditional Joy

Within the peace of my being, a liveliness flows.

Within the experience of this, is such a pervasive sweetness.

It is the sweetness of calm, the warmth of safety, the strength of invincibility, the positivity of harmony.

Yet underneath all of this, is a subtle bliss born of the utter pleasantness of the peace.

This bliss has a sparkling effervescence to it. It wells up and fills the heart space.

It flows out from the heart to meet everything in creation. It is the bliss of being that brings pure joy.

This joy is not the result of any event or thought or any desire being fulfilled.

It is an unconditional joy that gives upliftment and glory to every moment.

Unconditional joy becomes the background for each moment of my day.

Affirmation

Residing in the bliss of being, I live unconditional joy.

True Appreciation

Bliss ~ Awe ~ Appreciation ~ True Appreciation

When I tune into the liveliness and pleasantness within the heart space,
the bliss that comes seems to spill over into everything I see.
A liveliness and vibrancy exists that makes every color more intense, every taste more exquisite,
and a sense of awe pervades everything I perceive.
I am in awe of everything. Every experience, every moment becomes fascinating.
Awe pervades this moment and makes me appreciate every aspect of life.
I appreciate everything, from nature to the complexity of a computer, to the simplicity of a sock.
Life becomes full of awe and appreciation.

Affirmation

I live in awe and appreciate all that is.

Gratitude

Bliss ~ Fullness ~ Gratitude

As I become familiar with the heart space as a portal into my being,
a bliss begins to be ever present.
It fills the background and the silence.
The entire spaciousness of the heart begins to fill with this blissfulness.
As I put my attention on it, what was subtle becomes intense.
I feel like my heart might explode.
A fullness fills the heart space, and I am in awe of it and of everything.
From this, I feel a tenderness and I feel so very blessed.
I feel deep gratitude for life, for the opportunity to share with others,
for every moment and everything that has brought me to this moment of fullness.

I am so grateful to have this life. I am so grateful for all the blessings of this life.

I cannot help but say,
"Thank you."

Affirmation

With a fullness in my heart, I give gratitude for everything.

Generosity

Bliss ~ Overflowing Fullness ~ Generosity

As this fullness in my heart expands, it seems to overflow.
In this overflowing fullness of my heart,
the only longing I have is to share this fullness with others.
Sharing increases the flow of Light and Love.
It is a giving to others that increases the fullness and happiness within.
I receive more than I give, so there is no block, no resistance to giving.
Nothing is lost in giving. Everything is gained.
This fullness makes for the greatest generosity
as it is my greatest joy to give, to serve, to love others.

Affirmation
From the overflowing fullness of my heart, my greatest joy is giving.

Radiance Healing

Bliss ~ Warmth & Light & Radiance ~ Healing ~ Radiance Healing

As I become more familiar with the subtle bliss and as it expands, I notice it flows.

As it flows, it radiates and this radiance has a warmth and light within it.

Radiating this warmth and light has a healing effect on my emotions. It heals the hurts.

It has a healing effect on my energies and on my body.

It creates a wholeness, where there was fragmentation and disconnection.

As I radiate this light and warmth to thoughts or situations or relationships, I notice a profound and transformative effect.

Affirmation

The radiance of my inner bliss and light heals all.

Total Forgiveness

Oneness ~ Forgiveness ~ Total Forgiveness

In the expansiveness and spaciousness of my being that I discover through exploring the heart space,

I begin to explore the boundaries of my being.

The expansiveness seems almost infinite. As I expand further and further, and explore more and more,

I begin to have a sense of everything being within this spaciousness of my being.

I am one with everything.

Then with each person I encounter, this sense of oneness transforms everything.

I cannot judge them. I cannot criticize them. They are me.

They are doing the best they can. I am no different.

I can completely let go of the past and let go of all judgments and know all is well.

I am free. I reclaim all the power I invested in my judgments of others.

I reclaim all the power I invested in letting others' behavior determine my thoughts and my inner experience.

I am free.

Affirmation

I release all judgment and I am free.

Full Compassion

Oneness ~ Unity ~ Compassion ~ Full Compassion

*As I explore this heartfelt sense of being one with others—
of there being essentially one heart and many minds—
then something interesting happens.
In the fullness of my heart and my being,
I cannot help but feel compassion for others.
This compassion is not an intellectual understanding. It is not trying to understand.
It is a flowing of my heart and a sense of oneness and knowing that the flow of compassion heals us both.
It is fullness flowing in total compassion—
a flow of Universal Love that comes spontaneously with this sense of oneness.*

Affirmation
Within the oneness of my heart, all compassion flows.

Final Words

May these words inspire you to live the love you are.

May these words move you to open your heart to the treasures of your being.

May these words serve to expand your awareness and align with the Divinity within.

May love be yours in every moment.

May you know the source of love.

May you know the course love takes in opening you to Reality.

May you know the goal of love and all the seeking you have had in life.

May you know love in all its facets and in its every aspect.

May love be your liberation from all suffering.

May love heal all in your life.

May love be your guiding star.

May you forever live in the happiness of love flowing through you and your entire life.

May you be blessed and remain in awareness of the Light and Love that you are.

May you be blessed and live in the radiance of Light and Love shining to you from everything.

May you be blessed and know the source of Love.

My greatest wish for you is that you discover how amazing you are and know you are loved. And keep your Light shining brightly.

May it be so.

Love and Light,
Dr. Paul

Resources

Spiritual Mentoring with Dr. Paul

Email: HeartBasedMeditation@gmail.com

Heart-based Meditation Training

www.heartbasedmeditation.com

Spiritual Mentoring Training Program

Become a spiritual mentor and a teacher of Heart-based Meditation

Experience Awakening the Heart

"A picture is worth a thousand words, and an experience is worth a million wise ones."

If you are excited about what you are learning in the book and want to experience it more directly, consider our Awakening the Heart Course. It is highly experiential and can guide you to a direct cultivation of the heart. It gives you concrete tools to make the learning practical.

What students have said about learning these tools...

"I feel like I have healed some of the biggest issues in my life through being able to heart center and be present to them in a new and curious way."

"My family and my relationships — everything has transformed as I have come to know who I am through the process of exploring the heart space."

"My whole attitude to life has changed through conscious reprogramming. I feel more joy than I have ever in my entire life."

If you want to learn more about the course, use the scan code below:

Make a Difference with Your Review

Share the Gift of Awakening the Heart

"The best way to find yourself is to lose yourself in the service of others." – Mahatma Gandhi

When we give with an open heart, we brighten not only our own lives but also the lives of others. Together, we can help more people discover the path to inner peace and joy. Would you take a moment to help someone like you—someone curious about awakening the heart but unsure where to begin?

My mission is to make awakening the heart simple and full of grace for everyone, and you can be a part of that mission. Most people rely on reviews when choosing a book. By leaving a review, you could guide someone toward a deeper connection with themselves and the Universe. It doesn't cost anything and takes just a minute, but your review could change a spiritual journey forever. To make a difference, simply scan the QR code below and leave your review:

If you love helping others and decide to share your experience, I thank you from the bottom of my heart!
Warmly,
Dr. Paul

www.ingramcontent.com/pod-product-compliance
Lightning Source LLC
Chambersburg PA
CBHW070734020526
44118CB00035B/1303